AYUB KHAN-DIN

Ayub Khan-Din studied drama at Salford College of Technology
and at Mountview Theatre School. After graduating, he joined
Tara Arts, appearing in numerous productions with them,
including *Tartuffe* at the National Theatre. His other acting
work includes playing Sammy in the film *Sammy and Rosie
Get Laid*, appearing in *Coronation Street* and playing the title
role in a film of Dostoyevsky's *The Idiot*.

His first play, *East is East*, was staged as a co-production
between Tamasha, the Royal Court and Birmingham Rep,
and opened in Birmingham in 1996. After its Royal Court run,
it transferred to the Theatre Royal Stratford and then to the
West End, winning the John Whiting Award, the Writers' Guild
of Great Britain Best West End Play and Best New Writer
awards. The film of *East is East*, with screenplay by Ayub
Khan-Din, won the British Independent Film Award for Best
Screenplay, BBC Asia Award, Evening Standard Best Film,
Empire Magazine Best Debut, Galway Film Fleadh Best First
Feature, and the Golden Spike at the Valladolid Film Festival
in Spain.

Other recent theatre work includes *Last Dance at Dum Dum*,
which opened in the West End and toured nationwide; *Notes
on Falling Leaves* (Royal Court); and the forthcoming *All the
Way Home*.

Ayub Khan-Din

RAFTA, RAFTA . . .

based on
All in Good Time
by Bill Naughton

NICK HERN BOOKS

London

www.nickhernbooks.co.uk

A Nick Hern Book

Rafta, Rafta . . . first published in Great Britain as a paperback original in 2007 by Nick Hern Books Limited, 14 Larden Road, London W3 7ST

Rafta, Rafta . . . copyright © 2007 Ayub Khan-Din
Based on *All in Good Time* copyright © Bill Naughton

Ayub Khan-Din has asserted his right to be identified as the author of this work

Cover image: Dinodia Photo Library

Typeset by Country Setting, Kingsdown, Kent CT14 8ES
Printed in Great Britain by CPI Bookmarque, Croydon CR0 4TD

A CIP catalogue record for this book is available from the British Library

ISBN 978 1 85459 993 3

Rafta, Rafta . . . was first performed in the Lyttelton auditorium of the National Theatre, London, on 26 April 2007 (previews from 18 April), with the following cast:

EESHWAR DUTT	Harish Patel
ATUL DUTT	Ronny Jhutti
JAI DUTT	Rudi Dharmalingam
ETASH TAILOR	Arsher Ali
JIVAJ BHATT	Simon Nagra
LOPA DUTT	Meera Syal
LATA PATEL	Shaheen Khan
VINA PATEL	Rokhsaneh Ghawam-Shahidi
MOLLY BHATT	Natalie Grady
LAXMAN PATEL	Kriss Dosanjh

Director Nicholas Hytner
Designer Tim Hatley
Lighting Designer Hugh Vanstone
Music Niraj Chag
Sound Designer Paul Groothuis

For
Buki, Isabelle and Amelia

xxx

RAFTA, RAFTA . . .

Characters

EESHWAR DUTT, *fifty-five*
LOPA DUTT, *his wife, forty-nine*
ATUL DUTT, *their son, twenty-two*
JAI DUTT, *their younger son, eighteen*

LAXMAN PATEL, *fifty*
LATA PATEL, *his wife, forty-five*
VINA PATEL, *their daughter, Atul's wife, twenty-one*

JIVAJ BHATT, *Atul's boss, thirty-nine*
MOLLY BHATT, *his wife, thirty-five*
ETASH TAILOR, *twenty-two*

Setting

*Bolton. Present day. The home of Eeshwar and Lopa Dutt
and their sons.*

*This text went to press before the end of rehearsals so may
differ slightly from the play as performed.*

ACT ONE

Scene One

The set is a cross section of a terraced house: two bedrooms, living room and kitchen. The living room is furnished with a mixture of worn pieces from the seventies and eighties. An industrial sewing machine sits in one corner, covered in piecework. A Hindu shrine sits above the fireplace, lit by small, colourful oil lamps. One door leads off to a small kitchen, another to the street. There is a set of stairs leading up to the bedrooms.

EESHWAR DUTT, fifty-five, and his son, ATUL DUTT, twenty-two, enter, struggling to carry a very large pan, used for food at Indian weddings. JAI DUTT, eighteen, and ETASH TAILOR, twenty-two, follow behind with another big pan. They are all dressed in wedding garb.

EESHWAR. *Chelo, yaar!* Take some of the weight, boy!

ATUL. I am!

EESHWAR. I may as well be carrying it myself!

ATUL. Oh, shut up . . .

ETASH. I hate to think how heavy these were when they were full!

JAI. You'd think there'd been a bloody famine, the way that lot attacked the grub, Dad!

EESHWAR. It was more like a UN relief mission than a wedding feast!

ETASH *and* JAI *laugh.*

JAI. What're we going to do with this lot, Dad?

EESHWAR. Freeze it! It'll be good for months, this.

ATUL. Couldn't we have picked these up tomorrow?

EESHWAR puts his pan down in the centre of the room and takes a break. JAI and ETASH carry theirs through to the kitchen.

EESHWAR. The Girl Guides are doing a skip-athon. I promised the vicar I'd have everything cleared up before we left.

JIVAJ BHATT, thirty-nine, follows, carrying two large tinfoil-covered platters. EESHWAR points the way to the kitchen.

Straight through, Mr Bhatt . . .

ATUL. I don't know why you asked him to come.

EESHWAR. He's your boss, yaar! You have to cultivate these people.

ATUL. He's a perv!

EESHWAR. Even pervs are important for business.

Close behind the men come LOPA DUTT, EESHWAR's wife, forty-nine, LATA PATEL, VINA's mother, forty-five, and MOLLY BHATT, thirty-five, the English wife of JIVAJ BHATT. They carry bags and extra large, covered platters.

LOPA. Well, don't think you're just going to leave it there!

LATA PATEL and MOLLY go through to the kitchen.

EESHWAR. I've only just got it in the room.

LOPA. It's not staying in here.

EESHWAR. Why would I leave a cauldron of food in the middle of the living room, woman?

LOPA. So you wouldn't have far to reach while you watched the television!

EESHWAR. I put it down to give him a rest.

ATUL. No, you didn't!

EESHWAR. The boy's weak!

ATUL. I am not!

EESHWAR. He's got no strength in his arms.

LOPA. You made your own son fetch and carry on his wedding day!

EESHWAR. There was no one else to help.

LOPA. Well, now you're rested you can take it into the kitchen.

EESHWAR. You don't have to tell me twice. I said that's what I was going to do.

LOPA. Though, where I'm supposed to put it all . . .

EESHWAR. Did you lock up behind you?

LOPA. You didn't stop to find out, did you?

EESHWAR. A straight answer's all I want.

LOPA. Yes, I did. And I took down the decorations, swept up, turned off the lights, paid the DJ and packed up what's left of the food.

EESHWAR. Waste not, want not.

LOPA. It won't keep.

EESHWAR. It's a crime to throw good food away.

LOPA. If it's not eaten in a week, it's going in the bin.

EESHWAR. I paid good money for that.

She walks through to the kitchen.

There are people starving in India!

LOPA. Well, there's plenty to eat in Bolton.

ATUL *smiles*. EESHWAR *bends and takes the side of the pan.*

EESHWAR. Well, don't just stand there, take the weight!

Front door.

LAXMAN PATEL, *fifty, and his daughter,* VINA, *twenty-one, wife of* ATUL DUTT, *are about to enter the house.* VINA *is dressed in traditional wedding garments.*

LAXMAN. Vina . . . wait a minute, before you go in . . .

> VINA *stops and turns.* LAXMAN *takes out an envelope from his pocket.*

Here.

VINA. Dad!

LAXMAN. Just a little something extra . . .

VINA. Atul won't –

> *She makes to push back the envelope, but he presses it into her hands.*

LAXMAN. Never mind Atul . . . take it . . . Don't tell him. It'll go towards getting you your own place.

> *She takes the envelope and puts it in her bag.* LAXMAN *looks up at the house, dismayed.*

Why he wants to bring you here, when you have a perfectly good room at home you could both use . . .

VINA. Because it wouldn't be right, would it ? A husband moving in with his in-laws. Atul's quite old-fashioned about things like that.

LAXMAN. But look at the place, it's tiny . . . And these streets –

VINA. He wants to do everything himself. He doesn't want to rely on you or his dad. We'll get our own place eventually. I'll be fine . . .

> *He takes her face in his hands gently and looks at her.*

LAXMAN. I just wanted to say . . . how proud I was of you today. You looked so beautiful. I couldn't believe it was my little girl.

VINA. Oh, Dad!

Smiling, she throws her arms around him.

Don't sound so sad . . .

LAXMAN. No, no, I'm not . . . I just want to make sure you're happy . . . You are happy?

VINA. Of course I am . . . Oh, come here –

She gives him another hug.

Don't worry about me . . . I've got everything I want. Atul's the best thing that's ever happened to me.

LAXMAN. I know, I know . . . I'm just being silly. Just don't forget, I'll always be here for you, OK? If you ever need anything? Anything at all. You just call . . .

VINA. I will.

LAXMAN. And don't forget your mummy, *bete* . . . She doesn't show it, you know what she's like . . . but she'll miss you very much, as well.

VINA. I know, Dad.

He hugs her.

LAXMAN. What am I going to do without my little Rani . . .

VINA. I'll come over and see you. I'm not going into purdah.

LAXMAN. I know, but I'll miss our little chats.

VINA. Me too.

LATA PATEL *comes to the front door.*

LATA. I wondered where you two had got to. Might have known you'd be somewhere yacking. Come in out of the cold, Vina.

VINA *goes through to the house.*

LAXMAN. Can't I have a quiet word with my daughter on her wedding day?

LATA. You're always having quiet words, the pair of you.

LAXMAN. Not now, Lata . . .

LATA. I'm just saying . . . You're going to be lost now she's married.

LAXMAN. Funny to think she won't be at home any more . . . It won't feel the same.

LATA. Well, you're just going to have to get used to talking to me again.

She turns and walks off into the house, followed a moment later by LAXMAN.

Living room.

EESHWAR *comes in from the kitchen in an exuberant mood. He's followed by* JIVAJ, ETASH *and* JAI, *who carry glasses and soda water.* ATUL *is sitting by the fire with* VINA, *showing her a BlackBerry.*

EESHWAR. Here he is! Come on, Mr Patel, join me in a peg!

LAXMAN. I'd like that . . . It is a wedding, after all.

LATA. Remember the time, Laxman.

VINA. Oh, Mum, let him have a drink.

EESHWAR. *Arrey!* Mrs Patel . . . Give the man a break. It's not every day you lose a daughter!

LATA *gives her husband a look.*

LATA. It'll be your head in the morning, and you won't have Vina to run about and nurse you.

She goes into the kitchen. LAXMAN *heads over to* EESHWAR, *who is pouring out the drinks.*

LAXMAN. Give me a damn peg, yaar!

EESHWAR. Good man! Have a burrah peg! Atul, you having a drink with me?

ATUL *is unsure. He looks at* VINA.

It's no good looking at Vina, you're a husband now . . .
Time you started making a few of your own decisions.

VINA *smiles at* ATUL.

ATUL. Erm, yeah. Yeah, all right, Dad. Just a small one.

EESHWAR. A small one?

JIVAJ. He'll want more than a small one on his wedding night!

LAXMAN. Do you mind?

JIVAJ. Sorry, Mr Patel, didn't mean anything by it.

EESHWAR. Of course he didn't. Every man needs a drink on
his wedding night. I did, I'm sure you did, Mr Patel, eh?
Atul's no different from any other man . . .

He gives ATUL *another look.*

Second thoughts, maybe you should have a large peg after
all, son!

He and the other men burst out laughing. ATUL *looks hurt
and embarrassed.*

ATUL. Actually, I think . . . I think, I'd much rather have a cup
of tea.

EESHWAR. What? Chai? On your wedding day?

ATUL. I don't think whisky agrees with me.

EESHWAR. I'm not asking you to have a discussion with it.

EESHWAR *laughs at his own joke and the others join in.*

JAI. Come on, Atul, man, don't be a wimp! Tell him he's being
a wimp, Vina.

VINA. I will not.

LAXMAN. If he doesn't want a drink . . .

EESHWAR. I just think it's a bit odd that he can't have a drink
with his father on a day like today.

ATUL. We had a drink this afternoon.

ETASH. He likes brandy and Coke.

EESHWAR. This is a man's drink. Come on, son, I've poured it now.

ATUL. Jai'll drink it.

JAI. Give's it here, Dad.

ETASH. We've got some brandy at home? I could nip over and get it?

ATUL. Tea's fine.

EESHWAR. A son of mine drinking tea on his wedding day!

VINA. We had lots of champagne today, Mr Dutt. Maybe he's had enough, eh, Atul? I know I have.

EESHWAR (*softening, to* VINA). I suppose so . . . I wish you'd stop calling me, Mr Dutt! You can call me Dad, now.

VINA. All right . . . I'll go an' make you some tea, Atul.

She gives him a peck on the cheek and heads off to the kitchen. The men watch her leave.

EESHWAR. You've given me a goddess for my house there, Mr Patel. There's no doubt about that.

JIVAJ. You've got a good girl there, Atul, mind you treat her well.

ETASH. I remember the moment he saw her, he said he wanted to marry her. Knew it right off, didn't you, Atul?

ATUL *is a bit embarrassed by the conversation.*

EESHWAR. I'll be proud to call her my daughter. Very proud. Shown me nothing but respect from the moment I met her.

LAXMAN. There are so many bad things to lead a good girl astray these days.

EESHWAR. *Han, han* . . . I agree. Though don't get me wrong, I'm not old-fashioned.

LAXMAN. It's well known in the community, you're a forward-thinking man.

EESHWAR. I'm all in favour of integration.

JIVAJ. But there are limits, Mr Dutt.

EESHWAR. Oh, yes, I draw the line at tattoos and primitive piercing.

ETASH, ATUL *and* JAI *laugh*.

LAXMAN. McDonald's! Always full of our young people?

EESHWAR. Ears, nose an' eyebrow at a pinch! But anywhere else is bloody jungley and I won't have it in my house or on my telly!

Kitchen.

The women put the food away. VINA *is putting the kettle on.* LATA *suddenly bursts into tears.*

VINA. Mum, what's wrong?

LATA *starts to wipe the tears away and blows her nose as* LOPA *and* MOLLY *make a fuss of her.*

LATA. My little girl is making her first cup of chai for her husband . . .

She starts to go again. VINA *laughs*.

VINA. I've made him tea loads of times!

LATA. It's different now. You're a wife. Oh, you don't understand. Only a mother can see it . . . Just you wait till you're a mother.

VINA. Mum!

LOPA. Don't worry, Mrs Patel, we'll look after her.

LATA. There are so many things I should have told her.

VINA. Oh, Mum, please . . .

LATA. Things a girl should know about her wedding night that only a mother can tell you.

VINA. Oh, don't embarrass me now, you've been so good all day.

MOLLY. Looks like we've got a blushing bride here, ladies!

LOPA. Leave the poor girl alone.

LATA. These things have to be said.

VINA. Mum, just don't go there, all right?

LATA. I knew nothing when I married your father.

LOPA. Who did? We watched the livestock and that was it . . .

LATA. It all took me by surprise. The shock of it.

LOPA. Girls are different today. They have agony columns and *Richard and Judy*.

VINA. We've even got Indian lesbians now.

LATA *is shocked*.

LATA. *Hai Ram!* Listen to this girl . . . This isn't a laughing matter! How do I know what you know or . . . or don't know?

VINA. Why didn't you ask me?

LATA. How can I ask you about that? Besides, you're always too busy chatting-shmatting to your father! When do you ever have time to talk to me?

VINA. My friends have told me all I need to know.

LATA. Which friends? Sudah? Nushi? Ha! Tramps, the pair of them. Who'll take them now? No one, I tell you. Soiled goods!

VINA. Oh, Mum, of course I know about sex. I may not have done it yet, but I've got the theory down pat, all right? Does that put your mind at ease?

LOPA. They teach them all these things in school these days.

LATA. Do they need to know so much about it? It's not like this in India, thank God.

VINA. Where do you think the *Kama Sutra* came from?

LATA. Yes – but we never did it!

VINA. There's one billion, ninety-five million, three hundred and fifty-one thousand, nine hundred and ninety-five Indians living in India. So someone must be doing it!

They laugh.

LATA. There's more to a marriage than just the . . . the hanky-panky.

VINA*,* MOLLY *and* LOPA *find this funny.*

MOLLY. That's all there is. So get your ground rules down fast, Vina.

VINA. What do you mean?

MOLLY. Men are led by what's dangling between their legs, love.

VINA*,* LOPA *and* LATA *laugh with embarrassment.*

Just you make sure it's on your lead and not some tart's. Know what I mean? Have your fun and games now, then put it on ration later.

LOPA. Oh, Molly! . . . Take no notice, Vina.

MOLLY. I'm not saying make him beg or owt. Just get him to a pleading stage. Works a treat for me with Jivaj. But never refuse a man point blank, because they'll take it out of your housekeeping money!

VINA*,* LOPA *and* MOLLY *laugh.*

LOPA. You've got a man who loves you, *bete* . . . that's what's important. Isn't it, Lata?

LATA. It's a long, slow death without it . . .

Living room.

The men are dancing to loud bhangra music, led by EESHWAR.

ETASH. Come on Atul, man!

JAI. Come on, our kid!

> ATUL *glances up at the dancers.* EESHWAR *starts some crowd-pleasing moves.* ATUL *shakes his head. The other men part and encircle* EESHWAR, *clapping.* EESHWAR *starts showing off – the centre of attention, and enjoying every second of it.* EESHWAR *calls out to* ATUL.

EESHWAR. *Chelo, puttar!* Come and dance!

ETASH. Your dad's got some moves, Atul!

LAXMAN. You put these young men to shame!

EESHWAR. At my wedding I danced three days non-stop! And he's not danced once yet! What does that tell you?

ATUL. That you were as big a show-off then as you are now!

> ATUL *ignores his dad. He's more interested in his BlackBerry.*

Kitchen.

MOLLY *stands by the door watching the men dance, as the others put snacks and things on plates.*

MOLLY. He's a good dancer for his age, Mrs Dutt.

LOPA. And he'd be the first one to tell you as well – not known for his modesty, my husband . . . Don't watch him! If he sees he's got an audience he'll make a bigger fool of himself!

LATA. Oh, Mrs Dutt!

LOPA. He ought to sit down and let someone else take centre stage. He should know better at his age.

MOLLY. It's a wedding! He's happy!

LOPA. You'd think he was the bridegroom, the way he's behaving.

LATA. He's allowed to celebrate.

VINA *starts to tidy up*.

LOPA. Vina! *Arrey*, go and sit down, it's your wedding day!

LATA. Yes, go and sit with Atul.

VINA. I've been sat with Atul all day! We're already sick of the sight of each other . . .

LATA. *Hai, hai, bhagwaan!* God forgive you for saying that on your wedding day!

The other women turn, shocked. VINA *laughs*.

VINA. It's a joke!

LATA. You can't joke about these things. It'll bring bad luck. Terrible tragedies occur when brides tempt the wrath of the gods.

VINA. Maybe in Bollywood, Mum, not in Bolton.

LOPA. I'll heat up some of these pakora and samosa.

MOLLY. Chelo, I'll help – those men will dance themselves a hunger.

LOPA. Especially with Shah Rukh Khan out there, leading the way!

They laugh.

LATA. *Hai, hai, hai!* So much food left.

LOPA. Better too much, than too little.

LATA. *Han!* This is true!

LOPA. Weddings! If we'd ordered less, people would've complained we'd scrimped on the food!

LATA. And you wouldn't hear the last of it!

MOLLY. I remember Shakuntala Agarwal's niece's wedding. All the roti ran out! It was her niece, mind, but Shakuntala still carries the shame around to this day!

LATA. *Hai bhagwaan!*

MOLLY. Had to move to Ramsbottom.

LATA. A wedding tragedy, see, Vina. It happens. Don't tempt fate!

MOLLY. Situation got that bad, people were accused of hoarding. In the end, they had to order takeaway!

MOLLY and VINA start to laugh. Even LOPA sees the funny side of it.

One hundred roti. From three different restaurants. Exact money only. No change given!

VINA. Well, we had a brilliant day and everyone had more than enough to eat and drink. So thank you.

MOLLY. It were a belting do, Mrs Dutt.

LATA. So many people! Such organisation!

LOPA (*apologetic*). No, it wasn't enough, it was all too small . . . Such a tiny hall . . . I wish it could have been more.

VINA gives LOPA a cuddle.

VINA. It was all we needed.

LATA. Everyone went home happy.

We hear a cry from the living room. EESHWAR falls over and goes flying against the sewing machine.

LOPA. *Hai Ram!* What now . . . ?

The women all rush in to see what the commotion is about.

Living room.

LOPA *finds the scene very funny as the men are trying to help* EESHWAR *up.*

ETASH. Help us shift the couch, Jai!

LAXMAN. Are you all right, Mr Dutt?

JAI. Up you get, Dad . . .

LOPA. What have you done now, you old fool?

EESHWAR. Don't just stand there laughing, woman!

JIVAJ. He took a tumble there, all right? Get up slowly, Mr D.

> EESHWAR *is stuck between the industrial sewing machine and the wall.* LAXMAN *and* JAI *are helping him out.*

LAXMAN. Easy with him. Slowly now, Mr Dutt, you may have injured yourself.

VINA. Atul, help your dad.

> ATUL *goes to help but* EESHWAR *waves him away.*

EESHWAR. Guilty conscience?

ATUL. What?

> ATUL *goes back to his seat.*

Oh, please yourself.

JIVAJ. Gently now, Mr Dutt.

EESHWAR. I'm all right, I say.

LATA. Listen to my husband, Mr Dutt – his brother is a registered Ayurvedic practitioner.

LAXMAN. He's got a clinic off the Mancunian Way.

LATA. Walk-in.

EESHWAR. I'm just caught on the foot-pedal. Mind that wire . . .

LOPA. If you've damaged my machine . . .

EESHWAR. I've done nothing . . . I'm the victim here. He tripped me up.

LOPA. Who?

EESHWAR. He did . . .

He points at ATUL. ATUL *can't believe he's just been accused.*

ATUL. I did nothing of the sort, Mum.

EESHWAR (*mimicking* ATUL). 'I did nothing of the sort, Mum.' Yes you did, just as I turned and did that last *jhatka*, you stuck your foot out and tripped me!

ATUL. Bollocks, did I!

LATA. Atul, language! You shouldn't speak like that to your father.

EESHWAR. Thank you, Mrs Patel, I'm glad someone speaks up for respect round here!

He looks at LOPA.

Just because I was having a good time!

LOPA. You're always having a good time.

EESHWAR. It's his wedding! Someone's got to enjoy it for him.

LAXMAN. I don't think Atul had anything to do with it, Mr Dutt.

JAI. Atul wouldn't do that, Dad.

EESHWAR. Well, if he didn't, he manoeuvred that puff round, so I'd knock it when I bent for that *jhatka*!

ATUL. What would I want to go and do a thing like that for?

EESHWAR. How do I know what's going on in your head? All I know is, I felt something trip me. And it came from your direction.

The others all murmur their doubts.

ATUL. It came from the direction of that whisky bottle, more like.

EESHWAR. Are you saying I can't hold my drink?

LOPA. You see, you big drunken fool, you tripped yourself up!

EESHWAR. I have never, in all the years that I have danced the bhangra, tripped myself up! I'm far too nimble for that.

LOPA. Nimble!

EESHWAR. My agility knows no bounds when it comes to dancing!

LOPA *starts to laugh.*

Fleet of foot! That's how I've been described! Fleet of foot, woman!

LAXMAN. I couldn't bend like that and get away with it nowadays.

LATA. It's his discs.

LOPA. I wish it were his.

The others laugh.

All that gyrating at your age . . . You ought to be ashamed.

EESHWAR. I'd put any of those Bollywood efforts you watch to shame!

LOPA. Ha!

JIVAJ. He would as well.

MOLLY. I was dead impressed, Mr Dutt. You put me in mind of Chunky Pandey in *Tezaab*.

LATA. You're very knowledgeable.

JIVAJ. That's why I married her.

EESHWAR. You should have seen me when I was younger, my girl . . . They said I had film-star looks!

LOPA. Who'd have thought I'd married Shashi Kapoor!

EESHWAR. I'm much better-looking.

LOPA. Pity you never earned his wages.

EESHWAR. Could Shashi Kapoor work at the factory all the hours God has sent?

LOPA. If he'd settled in Bolton, I don't see why not!

LAXMAN. I doubt it, for all his talent. And he's one of the greats, if not the greatest!

LATA. Such charm!

LOPA. Such looks!

MOLLY. I wouldn't have kicked him out of bed for chewing chapatties.

EESHWAR. I was tripped!

ETASH. Atul couldn't have tripped you, Mr Dutt, he were busy on the net.

EESHWAR. The bloody net!

He looks about at the group.

I ask you? What's wrong with the boy? I give up! Internet webbing on his skenning wedding day! You just got married, son!

ATUL. Oh, was that what it was?

He smiles at VINA. *She walks over to* ATUL *and puts her arm round him. They are obviously very much in love.*

VINA. It's a BlackBerry, Mr Dutt. I bought it him.

LATA. They're all doing it now. Tapping-shmapping!

EESHWAR. It's not normal.

LOPA. Nor is jumping round the room like a monkey at your age!

ATUL. It's a wedding present.

EESHWAR. My father bought me a water buffalo for my wedding. I didn't sit there milking it all night long!

LOPA. Oh, leave the boy alone.

EESHWAR. When I got married, I went wild! It was madness!

LOPA. Don't remind me.

EESHWAR. Life and soul of the party I was!

LOPA. So he tells himself.

EESHWAR. I wasn't playing on the bloody internet web!

LOPA. Wasn't invented then.

EESHWAR. Yes, I know . . . but what I'm saying is –

LOPA. Even if there had been, we had no electricity.

EESHWAR. The point is –

LOPA. Or running water . . .

EESHWAR (*frustrated*). The point is –

LOPA. I had to walk to the well.

EESHWAR. I danced all bloody night!

LATA. He's probably tired, Mr Dutt. It's been a long day. Weddings can take it out of you!

JIVAJ. Especially the wedding night!

He shares a dirty laugh with ETASH *and* JAI.

ATUL. Do you have to talk like that?

MOLLY. Yeah – shut up, you!

JIVAJ. Just a joke, Atul, keep your hair on!

ATUL. I don't find that sort of thing funny.

EESHWAR. Eh, mind how you speak to your guests.

ATUL. It's my wedding.

EESHWAR. It's my house, and until you're living under your own roof you'll treat anyone I invite back here with a little more respect!

ATUL. All this 'cause I don't want to bloody dance!

EESHWAR. I want you to have a good time, putter! I just don't understand why you won't dance!

ATUL. Look, it's simple. I don't like bhangra dancing!

EESHWAR. What d'you mean, you don't like the bhangra?

ATUL. I'm not fussed.

LOPA rolls her eyes and sits back in resignation.

EESHWAR. It's traditional. It's part of your culture!

ATUL. You said yourself you've no problem with integration, 'adapt or die' you've always told us . . . If it doesn't work, lose it.

EESHWAR. I didn't mean the bloody bhangra!

He turns to LOPA.

This is all your fault!

LOPA. How?

EESHWAR. Books and bloody Beethoven . . . You've made him into a skenning . . . mardy arse!

VINA. I read as well, Dad . . .

EESHWAR. I know you do, my dear, and that's very good for a young woman who's just become a wife and has no children yet . . . but he's always bloody at it.

LOPA. He's never understood why Atul reads so much.

LAXMAN. Reading broadens the mind, expands your horizons.

EESHWAR. He's just a bloody cinema projectionist – no offense, Jivaj.

JIVAJ. None taken, Mr D.

EESHWAR. He doesn't need any more bloody horizons!

LAXMAN. Nothing wrong with ambition, Mr Dutt.

EESHWAR. Nothing at all. But you've got to start off happy with what you have. He's never happy about anything. Six jobs he's had so far!

ATUL. I'm feeling things out.

EESHWAR. What's to bloody feel?

LOPA. Do you have to swear on their wedding day?

EESHWAR. Etash, tell me, are you happy being an assistant projectionist?

ETASH. Yeah. It's all right . . . Get free tickets and that . . . Popcorn . . . Seen the odd Bollywood movie star.

EESHWAR. And you, Jivaj? It's been good to you, hasn't it? I mean, you're a boss of three cinemas now? Practically a captain of industry?

JIVAJ. I can't complain . . .

EESHWAR *looks at* ATUL.

EESHWAR. So why can't you be happy?

ATUL. I just don't want to be a projectionist all my life.

EESHWAR. I've worked in the factory, all my life!

ATUL (*exasperated*). I want something better.

EESHWAR. Better! I brought you up on what I earned from that factory!

ATUL. I want something different for my family.

EESHWAR. Family is it now? *Arrey decko!* He's talking about raising a family, and he's not had a proper job since he left school!

LOPA. All this because he wouldn't dance?

EESHWAR. What I could've done with your education!

ATUL. Nothing stopping you now, is there?

EESHWAR. You think I'm funny? *Han?* Do you?

VINA *tries to calm the situation.*

VINA. Some people just don't like to do certain things. With Atul it's the bhangra.

EESHWAR. How can he not like bhangra dancing! It's like saying you . . . you don't like curry!

ATUL (*enjoying the situation*). Well, now you come to mention it – nothing too spicy!

LOPA. Atul!

EESHWAR. I give up!

EESHWAR *goes to the mantelpiece and takes a pipe and a pouch of tobacco. He sits at the table and prepares his pipe.*

What's the world coming to when a young man . . . my son, a, a, son of mine . . . my eldest boy . . .

LOPA. We know who he is!

The others laugh.

EESHWAR. Would rather tap away at a skenning computer on his wedding night than . . .

LOPA. Watch his drunken father make a fool of himself?

LAXMAN. Nothing wrong with knowledge, Mr Dutt.

EESHWAR. Well, it's not knowledge that's got me where I am.

LOPA. That's one thing we can all agree on!

EESHWAR. You can laugh all you like, woman, but I came to this country with nothing but a cardboard suitcase and the best friend a man could ever want.

ATUL. Here we go.

LAXMAN. Never turn your nose up at another man's experience unless you wish to meet the same fate.

EESHWAR. Brijesh Kapadia.

LOPA. Do you have to bring him up tonight?

EESHWAR. Why shouldn't I? He was my best friend.

LOPA. Well, no one else knows him or wants to hear about him.

JAI. I do. Who were he, Dad?

LOPA. Nobody.

EESHWAR. Don't say that, Lopa. I know you never always saw eye to eye with Brijesh.

LOPA. We haven't seen him for years, and now you want to bore everybody with your stories.

EESHWAR. It's all I have of him now.

JAI. Go on, Dad . . .

LOPA. Don't encourage him.

JAI. I'm asking my dad, not you.

LOPA. And I'm answering for him.

JAI. Ooooo! You standing for that, Dad?

EESHWAR. No, I'm bloody well not. I knew him, Lopa, and so did you.

EESHWAR *pours himself another drink*.

He was closer to me than any other man I've ever known.

LOPA. I'll go and get the tea – we're going to need it!

LOPA *goes to the kitchen.*

EESHWAR. Inseparable, we were. Same village. Same school.

LAXMAN. I had a friend like that. We did in the old days.

EESHWAR. We worked the same fields, had the same dreams. We came to England together. What an adventure!

LAXMAN. You needed a good friend. Those were hard days for us.

EESHWAR. Scared stiff, we were. We'd never seen anything like it. Hadn't a clue where we were going, what we were going to do. But we had each other. My God, it was all so different! The people, the sounds, the smells. It seemed that everything we did was in total confusion! We always seemed to be sat in bus stations or railway stations, waiting. Always waiting to get somewhere . . . People staring . . .

LAXMAN. I just remember being wet all the time.

EESHWAR. We had nothing, did we?

LAXMAN. Not even a welcome!

EESHWAR. It was the first time in my life that I was made to feel different . . . It was so shocking. It's hard to explain now, but it was the look people gave you.

JIVAJ. They still give it you now.

EESHWAR. No, it was different then. I know what you mean, but . . . it's what was behind the look, in them days. It went straight through you.

LAXMAN. He's right.

EESHWAR. You could be walking down the street minding your own business, and one person would give you that look . . . I tell you how it made me feel, it made me feel like I was nothing.

He shakes his head as he remembers, and sips his whisky.

I'm not ashamed to say, it upset me. Deeply. I could never understand how people could be so cruel . . . I still don't. It's as if . . . as if it wasn't just me they were looking at. It was my family, my life, my whole world, they were dismissing . . . But Brijesh was there, he knew . . . he knew who I was . . .

EESHWAR *looks at* ATUL.

JAI. Where's he now, Dad?

EESHWAR. Oh, I don't know.

Beat.

People move on, you lose touch . . .

He claps his hands and rises.

Hey! Come on, yaar! This is a wedding! We've not had a song yet!

EESHWAR *starts to sing a cheeky Indian wedding song. The others laugh and join in.* ATUL *and* VINA *look a bit embarrassed. The others enjoy their embarrassment.* LOPA *comes in with a tray of tea things.*

LOPA. That's enough of that. Can't you see you're embarrassing the poor things?

EESHWAR. I'm serenading them.

JAI. It's only a bit of fun, Mum.

LOPA. It's crude. Your father should know better.

JIVAJ. It's a traditional wedding song, Mrs Dutt.

LOPA. Don't talk rubbish. Help me clear a space for this tea. Atul, bring the other chairs over to the table. Come and eat something, everyone. Come, come . . .

EESHWAR. Come along now, plenty to go round.

JIVAJ *and* MOLLY *help to clear the table as* ATUL *brings some more chairs. Everyone helps themselves to food and settles down.*

LOPA. Jai, get your father the harmonium. If he wants to sing, he can sing a proper song.

EESHWAR. That's very kind of you.

LOPA. And I mean something proper.

JAI *pulls an harmonium from a cupboard and brings it over to* EESHWAR, *who removes its dust cover.*

LAXMAN. That's a lovely instrument you have there, Mr Dutt.

EESHWAR *pulls out a handkerchief and lovingly gives the surface of the harmonium a wipe-down.*

EESHWAR. She's a beauty, isn't she? It belonged to my friend, Brijesh . . . left it here and never came back for it. Now he could sing, *ba pre ba*, what a voice that boy had!

LOPA. Yours is just as good, Eeshwar.

EESHWAR. Not like his, though . . . You've got to give the man his due, Lopa, he could sing a song.

LOPA. I suppose so.

EESHWAR. It was the stillness in his voice. He could stop time with it, eh na, Lopa?

LOPA. Mmm . . .

EESHWAR. The sound seemed to come from nowhere and fill the whole room . . .

EESHWAR *goes through the scales on the harmonium. Humming at first, gently adding more voice.* LOPA *starts to light the little candles around the shrine.*

LOPA. Jai, turn out the lights, let's pretend we're back in the village.

JAI *goes over and switches off the lights.*

EESHWAR (*singing*).
    Rafta, rafta vo meri, hasti ka saamaan ho gae.
    Rafta, rafta vo meri, hasti ka saamaan ho gae.

Pahale jaan, phir jaan-e-jaan.
Pahale jaan, phir jaan-e-jaan.
Phir jaan ne jaanaa ho gae.
Rafta, rafta vo meri, hasti ka saamaan ho gae.

JAI, ETASH *and* JIVAJ *quietly creep out of the room and up the stairs, as the others sit listening to* EESHWAR.

Din-ba-din badhati gayi, us husni ki raanaaiya.
Din-ba-din badhati gayi, us husni ki raanaaiya.
Pahele gul, phir gulbadan.
Pahele gul, phir gulbadan.
Phir gul, badhaanaa ho gaye.
Rafta, rafta vo meri, hasti ka saamaan ho gae.

Before EESHWAR *can start the next verse,* ATUL *suddenly starts to sing the notes of the song in qawwali style. The sound comes from nowhere, and takes* EESHWAR *and the others by surprise.* EESHWAR *is put out, but continues to play the harmonium, as* ATUL *now sings the last verse.*

ATUL.
App to nazadeek se.
App to nazadeek se.
Nazdeekar tar aate gaye!

LOPA.
Kya baat hai!

LAXMAN.
Wah! Wah! Wah!

ATUL *looks at* VINA *as he sings.*

ATUL.
App to nazadeek se.
App to nazadeek se.
Nazdeekar tar aate gaye!
Pehele dil, phir dilruba,
Pehele dil, phir dilruba,
Phir dil ke mehamaa ho gaye!

JIVAJ.
Kya baat hai!

LAXMAN.
Subhan allah! Subhan allah!

ATUL.
Rafta, rafta vo meri, hasti ka saamaan ho gae.

Everybody applauds ATUL, *who just looks embarrassed.*

LATA. That was wonderful, Atul. Very beautiful.

VINA *gives* ATUL *a squeeze.*

VINA. I told you he could sing.

MOLLY. He's a cross between Kishore Kumar and Mohammed Rafi. But definitely favouring Rafi.

LAXMAN. He obviously gets it from his father.

EESHWAR. Well, it isn't his timing he got from me, that's for sure.

LOPA. What's that supposed to mean?

EESHWAR. Well, he could have waited till I'd finished.

LOPA. Oh! Don't be such a big baby!

Everyone laughs. EESHWAR *looks at* ATUL.

EESHWAR. There are protocols for these things. Now, if you'd said at the beginning you'd like to join in . . .

LOPA. Sometimes, Eeshwar, you really make me . . .

EESHWAR. How was I to know he wanted to sing? For all I knew he'd given it up with the bloody bhangra!

MOLLY. But it were lovely him joining in like that, Mr Dutt. Like something from a film.

LOPA. He didn't like the competition . . .

EESHWAR. Competition . . . from Atul?!

ATUL. Thanks . . .

EESHWAR. I don't mean it like that, son. I've just had more experience than you. The . . . the timbre of my voice has matured over time.

LOPA. The what?

EESHWAR. You have a certain purity, I admit . . .

ATUL. Big of you to say so . . .

EESHWAR. But there is no substitute for age and experience!

  JAI, ETASH *and* JIVAJ *appear at the foot of the stairs. They are still laughing.*

MOLLY. Missed a treat, you lot, should have heard Atul sing!

LATA. Wonderful . . .

LOPA. Where have you been?

  EESHWAR *starts to put the cover back on the harmonium.*

JAI. Nowhere . . .

EESHWAR. Pop that light on, *puttar*. We'll play the elbow game!

LOPA. Not tonight, Eeshwar.

JAI. I'm not playing with him!

LATA. Another song, please.

MOLLY. Don't stop now, Mr Dutt.

EESHWAR. No, no, that's enough for tonight. Shouldn't strain the voice.

JAI. And we don't want the neighbours voting BNP.

ETASH. What's the elbow game?

EESHWAR. You don't know the elbow game? In my day we used it to sort out our differences.

LOPA. It's childish.

EESHWAR. It's a show of strength, without the need to resort to violence!

JIVAJ. I'll give you a go, Mr D.

JAI. Watch him, Jivaj, his hands are strong. He cuts through chapatties with his little finger!

EESHWAR. Save the jokes, boy, and watch a master at work. Over here, Jivaj! Come on, shift this lot . . .

EESHWAR goes over to the table and he, ETASH, JIVAJ *and* JAI *start to push the tea things to one side.* LATA *and* LOPA *put them on the tray.* EESHWAR *sits down and rests his elbow on the table.* JIVAJ *sits opposite him.*

Now, I'll give you a word of advice . . .

ATUL *and* JAI (*mimicking* EESHWAR). 'It's a game of chess.'

EESHWAR. Ignore them . . . But this isn't about brute force . . . It's a game of chess! Eye contact! Watch the eyes of your opponent . . .

He makes a gesture from his eyes to JIVAJ*'s. This again is mimicked by* ATUL *and* JAI.

They'll tell you everything you need to know. OK, take a hold.

JIVAJ *takes* EESHWAR*'s hand. They settle into position.*

OK. Ready?

JIVAJ. Yeah.

ETASH. All right, Mr Patel, could you referee, please?

LAXMAN. I've no idea what the rules –

EESHWAR. Just say 'Go'.

LAXMAN. All right . . . Are you both ready?

EESHWAR. Yes.

JIVAJ. Yeah.

LAXMAN. OK. Go!

> EESHWAR *suddenly slams* JIVAJ*'s hand down to the table.*
> JIVAJ *winces in pain and pulls his hand back.*

JIVAJ. Ouch! Bloody hellfire!

EESHWAR. Weren't expecting that, were you? I gave you the cobra! I told you, watch the eyes! See that, Lopa? Gave him the cobra! *Tharak!*

> EESHWAR *emulates a cobra striking.*

The cobra! Just like that! Who's next? Any takers? Etash?

ETASH. No thanks, Mr Dutt.

EESHWAR. Mr Patel, do you want to give it a go?

LAXMAN. No, I was never very good at it. Weak wrists.

EESHWAR. What about you, Atul?

ATUL. Wouldn't want to rain on your parade twice in one night, Dad!

EESHWAR. The man hasn't been born yet who can beat me at the elbow game.

> *The others laugh.*

ETASH. Look out, Atul.

JAI. Pappadoms at dawn, I think!

JIVAJ. Come on, Atul, show your new wife how strong you are.

MOLLY. Don't be daft – he wouldn't stand a chance with his dad.

JIVAJ. He's got youth on his side.

JAI. He couldn't take me, Dad. He never could.

ETASH. He's got wrists of steel, Atul has. I've seen him carry six cans of film up a flight of stairs.

EESHWAR. Ha! He couldn't even carry a pan of rice earlier. Had to put it down, he were so weakened.

ETASH. Go on, Atul, take him.

EESHWAR. Surprised he had enough puff to sing!

ATUL. All right, you asked for it!

    ATUL *gets up and heads for the table*.

LOPA. Atul, no. Now stop this silliness. Sit back down.

EESHWAR. It's only a bit of fun.

    LOPA *looks at* EESHWAR.

LOPA. You ought to know better.

LAXMAN. I'll put a fiver on Mr Dutt to win.

LATA. You will not!

VINA. I'll take that, Dad!

LATA. Vina!

VINA. I'm backing my husband, Mum.

EESHWAR. You'll lose that.

VINA. We'll see.

EESHWAR. Don't say I didn't warn you.

JIVAJ. I'll hold the stakes and I'll have a fiver on Mr Dutt.

EESHWAR. Anyone else want to lose some money tonight?

LOPA. No good ever comes from any challenge between father and son.

EESHWAR. Are you scared I'll beat him, Lopa?

LOPA. Stop showing off.

ETASH. I'm with Vina.

    JIVAJ *takes the money off* LAXMAN PATEL, VINA *and* ETASH.

JIVAJ. Looks like we've got a match on. Any more takers? Jai?

JAI *massages his father's shoulders.*

A fiver on the big man! Easy money, eh, Dad?

EESHWAR. Good boy! All right, ready when you are, Mr Patel.

EESHWAR *and* ATUL *take their grips.* ATUL *winces.*

ATUL. Hang on, you big cheat, you've got my hand gripped tight already!

EESHWAR. Well, you grip mine then.

ATUL. How can I, when it's already swallowed up by yours.

EESHWAR. That's the whole purpose of the game.

LOPA. If you're going to play, play fair, you big bully!

LOPA *tries to loosen* EESHWAR*'s grip. The others laugh.*

EESHWAR. What d'you think you're playing at, woman? Non-players off the green!

LAXMAN. She's right, Mr Dutt. Fair's fair.

EESHWAR. Who made you referee?

LAXMAN. You did.

EESHWAR. You're his father-in-law.

LAXMAN. And you're his father. Now, are you ready?

EESHWAR. Considering I've been nobbled by my wife . . . I suppose I am.

LAXMAN. Atul?

ATUL. Ready.

LOPA. Watch for the cobra, son. He always tries that first.

EESHWAR. Referee! She's giving my game away!

LAXMAN. Quiet please, Mrs Dutt. Ready . . . go!

ATUL *starts pressing. He forces* EESHWAR*'s hand almost down to the table. They are both straining. There is lots of support from both camps.*

JIVAJ. Bloody hell, I think he's got him!

JAI. Come on, Dad!

VINA. Come on, Atul!

LOPA. That's it, son!

ETASH. You've almost won.

LAXMAN *bends and looks at the players' hands to see if* EESHWAR*'s are touching the table.*

LAXMAN. He's holding by an inch.

JAI. He's not finished yet, are you, Dad?

MOLLY. Go on, Mr Dutt!

LOPA. You've got him beat now, son!

EESHWAR (*through gritted teeth*). Like hell I am, woman! Watch this!

EESHWAR *slowly and with tremendous effort starts to force* ATUL*'s arm upwards.*

JAI. Come on, Dad! Come on, you're doing it!

JIVAJ. *Chelo,* Mr Dutt. You can do it! Look at that! Look at it!

ETASH. Come on, Atul, get it down again!

LAXMAN. That's strength, that is.

VINA. Shut up, Dad. Whose side are you on?

LAXMAN. I'm impartial.

VINA. Come on, Atul, don't let him beat you!

EESHWAR. I've got him licked and he knows it.

LOPA. No, he's not. Not yet. Come on, son.

JIVAJ. Atul, your head's going to explode if you strain any more.

VINA. Leave him alone. Come on, Atul. Atul! Atul! Atul!

ETASH. Atul! Atul! Atul!

ATUL slowly starts to push EESHWAR's hand back again. EESHWAR strains to keep it up.

LOPA. Go on, son, you can do it. Finish him off!

EESHWAR looks at LOPA.

EESHWAR. Finish me off, is it, woman?

With one more tremendous effort EESHWAR pushes ATUL's hand back. There are more loud cheers of support. Suddenly with a loud grunt, EESHWAR slams ATUL's hand down on the table. ATUL pulls it away in pain. There are cheers for the winner and a round of applause. EESHWAR is enjoying every minute of it.

Who's bloody well finished now? Ha!

LAXMAN. That's a clear win. Well done, Mr Dutt.

JAI. Nice one, Dad!

LATA. That was very exciting.

MOLLY. Three cheers for the winner!

ATUL rubs his wrist. VINA tries to comfort him. But he shakes her off.

VINA. Are you all right, Atul?

ATUL. Yeah . . . I'm fine.

EESHWAR. Told you you'd lose your money on him. Best man won, eh?

LOPA. Oh, stop your crowing, you bighead!

ETASH. You nearly had him then, Atul.

EESHWAR. No real strength in his grip.

LOPA. He almost beat you.

EESHWAR. I used the python on him . . . The long slow squeeze!

LAXMAN. It was a near thing, Atul. Well done.

EESHWAR. Thought you had me licked, didn't you? I was slowly squeezing the strength from you all the time. The python . . . never fails.

LOPA. Oh, shut up. You and your snakes! Look at the size of your hands to his.

EESHWAR (*justifying his win*). I'm twice his age, aren't I?

LAXMAN. It's late, we'd better be going.

LATA. My God, it's two-thirty already.

EESHWAR. Don't go yet! There's still whisky in the bottle.

LOPA. He never knows when to call it a day. I'll get your coats.

MOLLY. I'll get ours as well.

EESHWAR. Jivaj-ji, one for the road at least?

LAXMAN *holds his arms out to* VINA.

LAXMAN. Come here and give your dad a goodnight kiss.

VINA *gives him a hug and a kiss*.

LATA. Put her down, she's a married woman.

LATA *gives* VINA *an awkward hug and kisses her on the cheeks*. ATUL *shakes his father-in-law's hand*.

Go . . . you and Atul, get off to bed now.

LAXMAN. Yes, you look tired. It's been a long day.

LOPA *hands over the coats*.

LATA. I'm just saying, Mrs Dutt. They should go and get some sleep.

VINA *and* ATUL *both look embarrassed.*

LOPA. Yes, go on, the two of you. Slip off now . . .

VINA. I don't mind helping to clean up . . .

LOPA. I'll sort it out. Eeshwar and Jai can help . . .

ATUL. Come on, Vina . . .

ATUL *and* VINA *head for the stairs. They are spotted by* JAI.

JAI. Creeping off without saying goodnight, Atul?

LOPA. Yes, they are, and we don't want any cheekiness from you.

JAI. Wouldn't dream of it, I just want to say goodnight to my new sister-in-law.

He gives her a kiss on the cheek. ETASH *and* JIVAJ *give her a kiss as well.*

VINA. Goodnight, everyone!

ATUL. Goodnight all!

LOPA. God bless!

VINA *and* ATUL *disappear up the stairs, watched by their guests and family. For a moment nobody says anything.*

LAXMAN. Right then . . .

LATA. Yes.

LOPA. You're coming to eat next week.

LATA. I'm looking forward to it.

EESHWAR. So are we, aren't we, Lopa? I said to Lopa only the other week, we don't do enough entertaining in this house. Well, now we've no excuse.

LOPA. Safe journey home. Bye-bye.

EESHWAR and LOPA *walk the* PATELS *to the door.*

LAXMAN *and* LATA. Bye. / Goodnight.

MOLLY *gives* JIVAJ *a nudge.*

MOLLY. Come on, you.

JIVAJ. I've not finished my whisky.

MOLLY. Yes, you have.

ETASH. I'd better be going as well.

They go, leaving LOPA, EESHWAR *and* JAI *alone in the living room.*

JAI. I'm off to bed. then.

He gives LOPA *a kiss and she ruffles his hair.*

LOPA. Goodnight, *beta*. God bless.

JAI. Night, Dad! You were brilliant tonight! The python! What a move . . .

He heads up the stairs.

EESHWAR. Goodnight, son! Maybe I'll teach it to you one day.

EESHWAR *wanders over and retrieves his drink.*

Now, that's what I call a successful wedding!

LOPA *gives him a dirty look.*

What have I done now?

LOPA. You know what you've done . . . Did you have to beat the boy on his wedding night. In front of Vina and everyone?

EESHWAR. It was just a bit of fun, a bit of entertainment for everybody.

LOPA. Would you have liked your father to have done the same to you?

EESHWAR. It was just a game.

LOPA. Was it? Was it just a game?

EESHWAR. Of course it was.

LOPA. You know Atul . . . he's not like Jai. He takes these things personally.

EESHWAR is genuinely concerned.

EESHWAR. You don't think I'd do anything to deliberately hurt him, do you?

LOPA. You just don't think sometimes, Eeshwar.

EESHWAR. I wouldn't want him to think I did it on purpose.

LOPA. Why does it always look like you take pleasure in hurting him, then?

EESHWAR looks guilty and lost.

EESHWAR. A bit of friendly goading . . . That's normal between a father and son . . . it's expected. D'you really think I hurt his feelings, Lopa?

He goes over to the stairs. He thinks for a moment.

(*Shouting.*) That was a good match, that, Atul.

Beat. LOPA watches him affectionately.

If I'm honest . . . I'd say you nearly had me there! Best opponent I've had in a while . . . Hard luck you lost.

VINA. Goodnight! Goodnight, Mr Dutt!

EESHWAR. Goodnight, *bete*, and God bless! God bless the pair of you!

He comes back into the room and sits at the table.

He didn't say anything.

LOPA. Probably sleeping, it's been a long day. But that was nice, what you said.

EESHWAR. I always try and do the right thing, but it always turns out bloody wrong.

LOPA. You need to get to know him more . . . Spend time with him. Show an interest.

EESHWAR. I will, Lopa . . . I'll try.

She rubs his back gently.

LOPA. *Chelo* . . . Let's go to bed. It's been a long day for everyone.

She heads for the stairs, EESHWAR *follows. He turns out the light.*

ATUL*'s bedroom.*

VINA *stands at the door. She has her nightclothes over her arm and she carries her wash bag.* ATUL *stands by the window, still in his wedding clothes.*

VINA. It was nice of your dad to say that.

ATUL. Yeah . . . He didn't have to, did he?

VINA. Why didn't you say goodnight to him?

ATUL. I don't know. I wanted to, but I couldn't.

VINA. You nearly beat him, you know.

ATUL. I think I could've . . . didn't seem right somehow.

VINA. Why?

ATUL. Dunno . . . It were the struggle in his face . . . in his eyes. I've never seen him look like that before. It's like he were looking at someone else . . . Did you see it?

VINA. No, I was too busy shouting for you.

ATUL. Made me feel weird, it did.

Beat.

VINA. He was the life and soul of the party today.

ATUL. He's well-liked round here. Even the ones who voted BNP like me dad.

VINA. Spent time with everyone today, he did. I was dead impressed.

ATUL. I wished I was more like him sometimes. You know – talking to people and that.

VINA. You weren't shy when you met me.

ATUL. I know.

VINA. You were very romantic.

ATUL. It had to be all or nothing with you.

VINA. Were you that sure?

ATUL. I knew I wanted to marry you. The moment I saw you in Bombay Talkie Videos.

She laughs.

I'd never met anyone with a knowledge of *Pakeeza* like you.

VINA. Was that all?

ATUL. Nor anyone as beautiful.

VINA. I feel dead strange, standing in here with you alone.

ATUL. So do I . . . like when I kissed you that first time.

VINA. I'd never been kissed like that before.

ATUL. I'd never kissed anyone like that before . . .

He approaches her and holds her. He reaches up and takes her face in his hands. He leans in to kiss her again. We hear the toilet flush in the bathroom.

JAI (*offstage*). Bog's free!

It breaks the mood. VINA *suddenly becomes shy.*

VINA. I'll just go and get changed . . . brush my teeth and that.

ATUL. All right . . .

She leaves. ATUL *looks about the room. He goes over to the wardrobe, opens it and takes out a vase of roses. He puts it on the bedside table. He stands there and thinks for a while. He takes off his wedding jacket. He looks nervous. He goes over to a record player and puts on a record. Dvořák's Ninth Symphony, second movement. There's a knock at the door. He goes over and opens it.*

It's all right, you can come in . . .

EESHWAR *walks in. He has on an old dressing gown over a pair of striped pyjamas.*

Dad . . .

EESHWAR. Just wanted to say, son. No hard feelings about tonight.

ATUL. Erm . . . no, Dad.

Pause.

EESHWAR. Because . . . you know . . .

ATUL. Yeah . . .

EESHWAR (*looking around*). Good . . . Everything all right? Vina settling in . . . ?

ATUL. Yes . . . fine.

EESHWAR *wanders over to the bed.*

EESHWAR. Glad I got this new bed for you . . .

He sits on the edge of the bed and gives it a little bounce.

Yes . . . more comfortable . . . bit more roomy, eh na? This is nice music . . .

ATUL. I thought you didn't like classical music . . .

EESHWAR. I'm not completely ignorant, you know. I've heard this one before, it's, erm . . .

He hasn't a clue who it is.

ATUL. Dvořák . . .

EESHWAR. Yes . . .

ATUL. Ninth Symphony? Second movement?

EESHWAR *still looks bemused.*

Hovis?

EESHWAR. Achaa! That's the one!

LOPA *appears at the door.*

LOPA. There you are! What are you doing in here?

EESHWAR. I was just checking everything was all right. That they had everything they needed . . .

LOPA. Out, come on . . .

We hear the toilet flush.

EESHWAR. Goodnight then, son.

VINA *appears at the door. She holds her dressing gown together.*

Hello, *bete*, I was just saying to Atul if there's anything you need. Let us know . . . We're just next door.

VINA. Thank you.

LOPA. Now, come on to bed.

EESHWAR *leaves the room.*

EESHWAR. Just tap on the wall, we're right behind you. Any time of the night. I'm a light sleeper, I don't mind.

LOPA *grabs him by the arm and practically throws him through the door.*

LOPA. Goodnight!

She closes the door behind them. We hear them arguing outside.

What were you doing in there?

EESHWAR. You said to spend a bit more time with the boy . . . Show more of an interest . . .

LOPA. I didn't mean tonight!

VINA *looks nervous.*

ATUL. Sorry about that.

VINA. That's all right.

She sees the flowers and goes over to them.

Oh, Atul, they're lovely . . .

As she bends to smell them, her dressing gown falls open. ATUL *looks at her. She sees him watching her.*

ATUL. Sorry . . . I didn't mean . . .

VINA. It's all right . . . we're married now.

ATUL (*smiling*). Yeah . . .

He walks over to her.

VINA. We've no need to stop any more.

ATUL. I know.

Beat.

I love you.

He kisses her, gently at first, then gradually more passionately. His shirt comes off and drops to the ground and she starts to kiss his torso. They slowly lower themselves down onto the bed. As VINA *falls back, the bed gives way and collapses with a crash.*

VINA *and* ATUL. Ahhh!

VINA *starts to laugh.*

ATUL. That frigging Jivaj Bhutt's done this!

JAI (*offstage*). Whey hey!

> ATUL *jumps up and starts banging the wall.* VINA *sits up and finds it all very funny.*

ATUL. Was it you, Jai, you little shit! Just wait till morning! I'm gonna bloody do you!

EESHWAR (*offstage*). Yes? Hello? Anything the matter?

> *Hearing* EESHWAR *sends* VINA *into convulsions of hysterical laughter.*

VINA. Are you all right, Atul?

> *She can't help but giggle.*

ATUL. Shut up! I've had enough of people laughing at me for one night!

VINA. Atul . . .

ATUL. Just shut up! You're as bad as the bloody rest of 'em!

> VINA *stops laughing, shocked at the state he has got himself into.*

Scene Two

ATUL*'s bedroom. Six weeks later.*

ATUL *is standing by the bedroom window looking out. It's not quite dawn and just a hint of light comes through the curtains.* VINA *is lying asleep in bed. He turns and looks at her.* VINA *wakes.*

VINA. What time is it?

ATUL. Early . . . go back to sleep.

VINA. How long have you been standing there?

ATUL. I couldn't sleep.

VINA. Come back to bed . . .

ATUL. It's no use.

VINA. Atul . . . why don't you go and see the doctor? You've been like this for the last six weeks . . .

ATUL *turns and looks at her.*

ATUL. No!

VINA. Maybe he can give you something . . .

ATUL. You mean Viagra?

VINA. No . . .

ATUL. Yes, you do.

VINA. I don't.

ATUL. That'll look good, won't it? Six weeks married and I'm asking for Viagra.

VINA. I didn't mean that at all . . .

ATUL. They don't just hand them out, you know . . . They want to know everything . . . all your business.

VINA. You don't need Viagra!

ATUL. Keep your voice down, will you? I don't want the whole house knowing about it!

VINA. You're the one shouting about it!

ATUL. You're the one saying I need it.

VINA. I'm not – look what you were like last year, at Holi. You were rampant. I had to fight you off. I couldn't look me dad in the eye when I got in.

ATUL. You should have let me do it.

VINA. We did everything but . . .

ATUL. At least we wouldn't be in this situation. You'd know there was nothing wrong with me.

VINA. I don't think that anyway.

She gets up and goes over to him.

It's all in your head.

ATUL. Is it? Is it normal to have a beautiful wife and not be able to do anything . . . ?

VINA. It's all about relaxing.

ATUL. I am relaxed. I'm relaxed when we start and then . . .

VINA. Atul, is it me? Maybe it's me you don't fancy any more.

ATUL. It isn't . . .

VINA. They say when you get married things change. You go off people.

ATUL. It's nothing like that. I . . . I just thought everything'd be different once we were married . . . I didn't think we'd still be stuck here with my parents for starters . . . Nothing's gone right from day one . . .

VINA. I don't care if we never do it.

ATUL. Not now, maybe, but you will one day. You can't have a marriage and not have that. It goes without saying.

VINA. My mum says there's more to marriage than just sex. And she should know, 'cause I've never heard her and my dad doing it.

ATUL. Old Indians don't make any noise.

VINA. I don't care about it . . . just as long as we're together.

ATUL. I don't think that'll be enough in the long run. If I can't give you this, what chance have I in doing anything else for you. You had everything with your mum and dad, now what've you got?

VINA. I've got you.

ATUL. Yeah . . . well, we've got nothing if we can't do that.

VINA. It doesn't matter.

ATUL (*irritated*). Of course it matters! What are people gonna say?

VINA. About what?

ATUL. They're gonna start wondering why you aren't pregnant soon!

VINA. No, they're not.

ATUL. They're Indian, of course they will. And when nothing's happening they'll start pointing their fingers at me.

Pause.

VINA. Maybe if you talked to a friend . . .

ATUL. Are you mad? I'd never hear the last of it . . . It's bad enough putting up with Jivaj Bhatt and his smutty jibes, as it is. You haven't told anyone, have you?

VINA. No . . .

ATUL. You don't sound so sure . . .

VINA. You know . . . it's just the usual jokes from the girls . . .

ATUL. When you say 'usual', I take it to mean this is a regular occurrence, ergo, you must have said something for them to keep on at you . . .

VINA *laughs*.

VINA. What are you talking about . . . ?

ATUL. I'm glad you find my predicament funny.

VINA. Atul, lighten up, will you . . . The more worried you get the harder it's gonna be – or not be, in your case . . .

She waits, not sure what his reaction will be. He smiles and laughs, she joins in. He holds her and kisses her.

ATUL. I knew there was a reason I married you.

VINA. And that is?

ATUL. You can still make me laugh.

He kisses her again, more passionately. Then he starts to kiss her neck, his hands move over her body. She lets out a sigh, and he responds to her moans. They move over to the bed. ATUL *gets on top of her and starts to push up her nightgown.*

VINA. Ohhh, gently . . . Here . . .

He's a bit clumsy, and VINA *reaches down and tries to help. The landing light goes on. She sees it and is not sure whether to stop* ATUL. *We hear* EESHWAR *coughing. He clears his throat loudly outside the door.*

Atul . . . Atul . . . No, don't, your dad . . . Ohhhhh . . . your dad's gone to the toilet.

We hear EESHWAR *urinating loudly and then he passes wind.*

VINA. Atul!

ATUL. What?

VINA. Your dad . . .

ATUL. What are you going on about him for now?

VINA. He were outside . . .

He angrily jumps up and starts to adjust his clothes.

ATUL. For God's sake, Vina! I was all set . . .

VINA. Not quite . . .

ATUL. What d'you mean, 'not quite' . . . ?

VINA. It wasn't . . . you know.

ATUL. It was.

VINA. Not enough . . .

ATUL (*angrily*). Since when did you become a bloody expert?

VINA. I've got a good idea when . . .

ATUL. I hope that's all you've got as well.

VINA. What's that supposed to mean?

ATUL. You seemed to be doing a lot of pulling and tugging . . .
I wondered if you'd done this before.

VINA. You know that isn't true.

ATUL. It makes me wonder if you want it at all.

VINA. Atul . . .

ATUL. What am I supposed to think? You laughed at me on
our wedding night . . . Now you're putting me off by going
on about me dad . . .

VINA *starts to get upset.*

VINA. I want to do it with you, you know I do. I've never
been with anyone else and I don't want to . . . I wanted you
to be my first.

ATUL. Well, you could have fooled me!

VINA. Atul . . .

*She reaches for him. He pulls away and sits on the side of
the bed.*

ATUL. Don't touch me, all right? Just don't . . . come near me!

He gets up and heads back over to the window. VINA *starts
to cry. We hear the toilet flush and the landing light goes
out, leaving them both in the early dawn light.*

Scene Three

Kitchen. Later that morning.

The remains of breakfast are on the table. LOPA *is pouring tea into a cup.* JAI *is quickly eating the last of his breakfast.*

LOPA. Slow down or you'll make yourself sick.

> JAI *jumps up and starts to put on a leather jacket.*
> EESHWAR *comes in and sits at the table.* LOPA *passes him his tea.*

JAI. Can you tell Atul to remember the complimentary tickets?

EESHWAR. You on a hot date tonight, son?

LOPA. He's taking Vina.

EESHWAR. And her husband has to supply the tickets!

> JAI *grabs his helmet from the sideboard. He jams another piece of toast in his mouth.*

JAI. Want a lift to work, Dad?

EESHWAR. Not on that thing, I don't.

LOPA (*smiling*). If you wait a few minutes, you can give me a lift to the shops.

JAI. No way!

LOPA. I'll wear a helmet.

JAI. Wear what you want, but you're not getting on my bike. I'm off. See you!

> *He gives* LOPA *a peck on the cheek and heads out of the door.*

EESHWAR. Bye, son. God bless you. There's one you don't have to worry about.

LOPA. Meaning?

EESHWAR. Nothing.

LOPA. You never say 'nothing' without meaning 'something'.

EESHWAR. Jai's already mentioned getting his own place and moving out. He's doing well at college, he's mobile, he's an independent sort. Yet His Highness the Maharaja of Bolton upstairs is still here with a wife.

LOPA. Oh, leave him alone.

EESHWAR. I've no problem with them being here. It's just that I'm being made to feel that I'm not welcome in my own home.

LOPA. Now you're being ridiculous.

> EESHWAR *goes over to the kitchen. He picks up a pair of boots. From a box on the sideboard he produces a boot brush and starts to give the boots a scrub.*

EESHWAR. It's all the bloody whispering. Every time I walk past their room it's 'wishy, pishy, wishy, tishy'! It's not right.

LOPA. They're newlyweds. All young people like a bit of privacy.

EESHWAR. There's something not right there, if you ask me.

> *He starts to put on his boots.*

LOPA. Nobody is.

> *Pause.*

EESHWAR. She doesn't sing any more these days, does she?

> LOPA *sits down at the table.*

LOPA. You've noticed that.

EESHWAR. I may not have your female intuition, Lopa. But I know when something's wrong in my house. And something is wrong in my house. She doesn't look you in the eye the same way . . .

LOPA. Shhh, someone's coming down.

EESHWAR. That girl's not happy.

LOPA *gets up and starts to clear the breakfast things.*
VINA *appears at the bottom of the stairs. She doesn't see*
EESHWAR *at first.*

LOPA. Morning, Vina. Can I get you some breakfast?

EESHWAR. Morning, *bete.*

VINA *pulls her dressing gown together.*

VINA. No thanks . . . I just wondered if it were OK to have a
quick bath.

LOPA. Of course . . . there's plenty of hot water left. Go and
run it and I'll pour you a cup of tea.

VINA. Thanks.

VINA *walks past* EESHWAR *to the bathroom, which is*
beyond the kitchen. EESHWAR *puts on his coat and heads*
for the door.

EESHWAR. I tell you, she's not happy.

LOPA. She's got a good husband.

EESHWAR. Just because he's a good son to you doesn't mean
he's a good husband to her. I'm telling you, something's not
right . . .

LOPA. Of course it's not. And it won't be until they have their
own house. Space to breathe, have a bath when they want . . .
Whisper when they want . . .

EESHWAR *stops and looks pensive.*

EESHWAR. You'd tell me if it was money they needed?

LOPA. Of course.

EESHWAR. I don't want to see them struggle, there's no point.
I . . . I could sort something out, not much . . . but it
would be something to get them started. Just don't tell

him I offered . . . Pretend it's from you. That would be best, I think . . . he's proud . . .

EESHWAR *suddenly seems very vulnerable. There is an odd silent moment of intimacy between them.* LOPA *gives his arm a gentle rub.*

LOPA. Go on, go to work or you'll be late. God bless.

EESHWAR *leaves through the front door.* VINA *comes back into the room.*

Are you not going to work today?

VINA. I've a half day.

LOPA. Then you should go back to bed.

VINA. My dad'll be up this way today, so he said he'd call round.

LOPA. Here, sit, have some tea.

VINA *sits at the table.* LOPA *pours* VINA *some tea, then starts to tidy up round the room.*

Sounds like Atul getting up.

VINA. I told him to stay in bed, he didn't . . .

LOPA *looks at her.*

He didn't sleep well last night.

LOPA. I thought I heard somebody moving around.

We hear the toilet flush upstairs.

VINA. I'd better go and have my bath.

She jumps up and heads for the bathroom. We hear ATUL *coming down the stairs.* ATUL *appears at the bottom of the stairs in his pyjamas.*

ATUL. Has he gone?

LOPA. Has who gone?

ATUL. Me dad.

LOPA. You just missed him.

ATUL. Where's Vina?

LOPA. Having a bath.

ATUL. Oh.

> ATUL *wanders over to the table. He helps himself to a bit of old toast. He picks up a discarded newspaper, flicking through it. He walks over to the sideboard, picks up a radio and starts to tune it. We hear the beginning of Elgar's Cello Concerto in E Minor, Op. 85. All this is watched by* LOPA.

LOPA. Breakfast?

ATUL. Just a cup of tea.

LOPA. Jai asked me to remind you about some free tickets.

ATUL. Did he?

> *Pause.*

LOPA. There's nothing wrong between you and Vina, is there?

> *This instantly gets his attention.*

ATUL. What? No . . . Why, has she said something?

LOPA. No. Only your dad noticed she wasn't singing and laughing like she used to.

ATUL. He said that?

LOPA. He might not seem it, but he can be sensitive to things at times.

ATUL. I just don't see the two words aligned somehow . . . 'sensitive' and 'Dad'.

LOPA. Well, he's picked something up and he knows something's not right. That girl needs a home of her own.

ATUL (*snapping*). Yes. Well, we both do. But until I can afford to rent something nice, we'll have to make do.

LOPA. Why don't you put your name down on the council waiting list?

ATUL. And get shoved in some ghetto? No, thanks. I'll decide where I live and who my neighbours are gonna be. And if that means I have to wait and buy my own place, I will do.

LOPA. So we're not good enough for you now?

ATUL. It's not that, Mum. It's this place . . . If I have kids, I want them to know there's something different beyond these streets.

LOPA. What are you going to show them if you're still sat here yourself?

ATUL. What's that supposed to mean?

LOPA. Well, you . . . you go on about your father working in the same place . . . living in this house all these years. Like he was nothing.

ATUL. I didn't mean it like that.

LOPA. How did you mean it? How is he supposed to feel?

ATUL. Oh, come on . . .

LOPA. Don't you ever forget what your father did . . .

ATUL *realises how angry she's getting.*

ATUL. Mum . . .

LOPA. Do you think it was easy for him? A young man from a village in the middle of nowhere, no education or money. Can you imagine what it was like to be thousands of miles away from your family . . . ? He did that, he made a choice to do something about his life. He came here. He brought me here . . . and he made us a home.

ATUL. No one's saying he didn't . . .

LOPA. It's exactly what you're saying. And I don't like it. He may not be perfect, but he's done a lot he can be proud of.

ATUL. And I haven't? Is that what you're saying?

LOPA. I've always supported you in everything you've done.

ATUL. That's not what I asked you.

LOPA busies herself clearing up the breakfast things.

LOPA. You'd better do something to cheer that girl up a bit.

ATUL. She'll be fine.

LOPA. Don't take that for granted, son, because one day she won't be.

ATUL. I'm going back up to bed.

He takes a step towards the stairs.

LOPA. Atul, you're a good boy. But you keep all these things wrapped tight inside. There's two of you now, you know . . .

ATUL. We'll be all right.

He heads off up the stairs, carrying the radio and his tea. LOPA stands for a moment after he's gone. VINA comes in carrying her teacup.

VINA. Is everything all right?

LOPA. Fine . . . everything's fine.

She goes back to clearing away the breakfast things.

He's gone back to bed. There's nothing wrong between you and him, is there?

VINA. No, why, has he said something?

LOPA. No, I just wondered.

LOPA starts to put on a coat over her sari.

Why don't you take up a fresh pot of coffee? Just for the two of you? The kettle's nearly boiled.

VINA. Do you think he'd like that?

LOPA. Of course he would. I've got some nice biscuits you can take as well. Now, where's my basket . . . ? Vina, I'm popping out, I won't be back for a while. I've some shopping to do, and Mrs Thakkur isn't feeling very well and I said I'd drop in and pay her a visit . . .

VINA. If you need some shopping, I don't . . .

LOPA. No. You make that coffee.

LOPA *picks up her basket and heads out of the front door.*

VINA *realises that this is her chance. She carries the pots through to the kitchen. She comes back through and opens her toilet bag. She pulls out a compact mirror and applies some lipstick. She brushes her hair, then takes out a small perfume bottle and sprays a little on her neck. She takes off her dressing gown, revealing a little more cleavage. She stands on a chair and tries to look at herself in a wall mirror, straightening the nightgown across her buttocks.*

Unbeknownst to her, JAI *has re-entered the room. He stands admiring her at the door.*

JAI. So this is what you get up to when you're alone.

VINA *is embarrassed and shy.*

VINA. How long have you been standing there?

JAI. Long enough.

VINA. Pass me that dressing gown, please.

JAI. Do I have to?

VINA. Jai!

JAI. All right, keep your hair on.

He smiles and, picking up the dressing gown, takes it over to her.

Just admiring the view.

She snatches it and slips it on.

VINA. If you weren't my brother-in-law, Jai Dutt, I'd –

JAI. You'd what?

He reaches up and helps her step down from the chair. For a moment they are very close.

VINA. I'd give you a thick ear . . . And I'm not alone. Atul's got a half day for a change.

She goes back to the kitchen. JAI *picks up her perfume bottle and smells it.* VINA *returns with a tray, cups and a coffee pot.*

JAI. One of them for me?

VINA. No, this is for a private tea party. And you're not invited.

She takes him by the hand and leads him to the door.

JAI. I'm very entertaining.

VINA. So you keep telling me.

He grabs a folder from the sideboard as he passes. She opens the door for him.

JAI. I can't believe you're chucking me out. I'm considered a catch round here.

VINA. I always throw the tiddlers back.

JAI. That hurts.

VINA *smiles.*

VINA. Go to work or I'll tell your mum.

JAI. I'm going!

She closes the door behind him and smiles. She goes through to the kitchen and takes the tray. She is about to go up the stairs when the doorbell rings. She is in two minds whether to answer. She puts down the tray, goes over and opens the door. LATA PATEL *bustles into the living room.*

VINA. Mum, what are you doing here?

LATA. Nice to see you as well.

VINA. I didn't mean . . .

LATA. Was that Jai I just saw leaving?

VINA. Yeah, he'd forgotten something.

LATA. Achaa . . . Has your father called round yet? He said he would.

VINA. No . . .

LATA. I've just had a call from India. Your Uncle Pershotum died.

VINA. Oh . . . I'm sorry . . .

LATA. You never knew him – he was your father's stepbrother. They hadn't spoken for years – disagreement about a water buffalo.

She looks about the room.

I'm glad I never ended up in one of these little streets. I suppose I should be thankful to your father for that.

She notices that VINA *is still in her nightclothes.*

Not dressed yet?

VINA. Half day.

Pause.

LATA. Mrs Dutt not here?

VINA. Her friend's not well. She went to visit.

LATA. Achaa . . .

Pause.

Just you and Atul then?

VINA. Yeah . . . I was just taking him up some coffee.

LATA. Coffee? . . . Smells nice.

VINA. He likes coffee.

LATA. Two cups?

VINA. I was going to have one with him.

LATA. I thought you preferred chai?

VINA. No. Coffee.

LATA. Achaa.

Beat.

VINA (*reluctantly offering*). Would you like one?

LATA. I don't want to interrupt anything. You young people need your time alone.

VINA. You're not. Sit down.

LATA *sits at the table, as* VINA *sets out the cups, resigned to entertaining her mother. She's watched closely by* LATA.

LATA. You look a bit pasty. Are you well?

VINA. I'm fine.

Beat.

LATA. You're eating well?

VINA. Yeah.

LATA. Not off your food at all?

VINA. No.

Pause.

LATA. Has Atul done anything about getting you your own place?

VINA. He's trying to sort something out.

LATA. Well, make sure you're careful.

VINA. We are – everything we earn goes in the building society.

LATA. I mean, careful you don't start something, before you have your own home.

VINA. Start what?

LATA. What else can you start?

VINA. Mum!

LATA. These things can happen. No matter how careful you are. When you're newly married the novelty is there, isn't it? The enthusiasm. Then before you know it . . .

VINA. Well, it won't happen to us.

LATA. It doesn't matter how you try to stop it. Nature will always find a way through. It always has done and always will. You're no exception. It's what it's there for, after all.

VINA. It'll have a job in our case.

LATA. Because you can't underestimate the pressure a baby can bring to you both, especially as you aren't settled in your own home yet. You know how you get when you can't get your own way, Vina. Remember the time when we had your Uncle Devdass and Auntie Putle over to stay and you had to give up your room –

VINA (*irritated*). I've got it sorted, all right? God! I'm not a child any more, Mum, I'm a grown woman, and I'm not pregnant! Believe me, I'm not bloody pregnant! Is that nice and clear for you? Or do you want me to spell it out to you in bleeding Hindi? I'm. Not. Pregnant!

LATA *is shocked by* VINA*'s outburst. She stands to leave.*

LATA. Well, if that's the way you take a bit of motherly advice . . . I'll go. I'm sorry I'm not your father. You'd listen to him, wouldn't you? Always got time for your father . . .

VINA *starts to cry.*

I . . . I just meant it would have been nice to sit and chat . . . We never used to . . .

VINA. Oh, Mum . . .

LATA *looks at her and realises something is wrong.*

LATA. What is it? What's wrong? . . . You have got yourself pregnant, haven't you?

VINA. No . . . I can't . . .

VINA starts to sob. LATA looks concerned but doesn't go to her daughter.

LATA. What do you mean? You're all right? There's nothing wrong with you?

VINA. No, I'm fine . . .

LATA. Is it Atul?

Pause

Vina?

VINA. Promise you won't say anything to anyone.

LATA. Of course I won't. What is it? Is there something wrong with him?

VINA. Nothing's happened, Mummy –

LATA is confused.

LATA. I . . . I don't understand, *bete*. Calm down and speak slowly . . .

VINA. Between me and Atul – nothing's happened . . .

LATA. How do you mean? Nothing . . .

Suddenly the penny drops.

Upstairs? Nothing's happened upstairs? . . . In your bedroom? On your bed? . . .

VINA. No.

LATA. Nothing at all? Think now . . .

VINA. No . . . I mean . . . you know, bits and pieces, but . . .

LATA. You mean he hasn't got around to – *it* yet?

VINA. No . . . not properly.

LATA (*loudly*). How do you mean, 'not properly'?

VINA. Shh, keep your voice down. No one's supposed to know!

LATA. Well, he either has or he hasn't?

VINA. We haven't had . . . intercourse!

> LATA *covers her face with her sari. She brings it down slightly so we see her eyes.*

LATA. You're still a vir –

VINA. Yes!

> LATA *tweaks her ear lobes.*

LATA. *Hai bhagwaan.*

VINA. Don't look at me like that . . . I'm not a freak. I don't want your pity. I'm sure it'll happen eventually . . .

LATA. Oh, *bete*, but if it doesn't . . . It could ruin your whole married life. It could ruin your life.

VINA. No, it won't. Things are different today . . .

LATA. That never changes . . . You haven't told anyone else, have you?

VINA. No!

LATA. Good. It'd be round the whole community in hours if it got out. My God, the scandal!

VINA. It's got nothing to do with anyone else and I'd like to keep it that way.

LATA. Not so much for you, *bete*, you're the innocent in all this . . . But for Atul! What people will say about him? Vina, you –

VINA. I don't want to talk about it any more.

LATA. It's not something you can keep to yourself.

VINA. No, no, I've said too much as it is. It's between me and Atul. Just forget what I said.

LATA. It's to do with both our families and we need to talk!

VINA *jumps up and starts to collect up the coffee things onto the tray.*

VINA. No! Stop it! I don't want to listen!

LATA. For once in your life you will listen to me. Atul has a responsibility, a duty. Until he's done it, he's not a proper husband and you're not a proper wife.

VINA. Stop it! Stop it! I wish I'd never told you now!

LATA. I'm telling you the truth!

VINA. I don't care, we love each other and that's all that matters!

LATA. That won't be enough to save your marriage!

VINA. You're enjoying this, aren't you?

LATA. Don't be stupid. I just want what's best for you.

VINA. You've never wanted what's best for me.

LATA. Vina!

VINA. You're happy something's wrong. Well, at least I've got a marriage, Mum . . . We might not have had sex yet, but at least there's love between us! Which is more that you've ever given my dad!

LATA *slaps* VINA *across the face. There's a knock at the door.* VINA *quickly wipes her eyes and takes the tray to the kitchen.* LATA *goes over to the door and opens it.* LAXMAN *comes in, carrying a briefcase.*

LAXMAN. Hello, what are you doing here?

LATA *says nothing. She walks back into the room.*

What's wrong?

LATA. Just wait till you hear . . .

VINA *comes in from the kitchen. She sees her father and rushes over to him, crying.*

VINA. Oh, Dad! Oh, Daddy!

LATA. No use turning to your father. He can't help you this time.

VINA *falls into his arms and he comforts her.*

LAXMAN. What's wrong, *bete*? What is it?

LATA. Ask her. Ask your little girl.

VINA. She says I'm not a proper wife. Oh, Dad . . . take me home. I'm so unhappy, I just want to come back home.

End of Act One.

ACT TWO

Scene One

Living room. Later the same day.

EESHWAR *stands at the table. He's polishing the harmonium.*
LOPA *sits at the sewing machine, working.*

LOPA. Shouldn't they have brought the television back today?

EESHWAR. I don't care if they never bring it back.

LOPA. I like it.

EESHWAR. Bloody telly! Bloody DVD! Bloody video! . . .
Bloody satellite dish! What's the point? All you ever watch
is bloody Bollywood! It's killing the art of conversation.

LOPA. Stop swearing.

The doorbell rings.

There's the door.

EESHWAR. Visitors?

He looks at her.

LOPA. No, don't move – I'll get it.

She gets up and heads for the door.

EESHWAR. Visitors? In the middle of the week? Whoever it
is, don't ask them in. I've got no time to sit about here,
yacking-shmacking about nothing . . .

LOPA *opens the door to* LAXMAN *and* LATA PATEL.

LOPA. Mr and Mrs Patel . . . This is a nice surprise . . . Aye,
aye . . . come in, come in. Eeshwar, it's Mr and Mrs Patel!

They enter, both looking a little nervous. EESHWAR *comes over and shakes* LAXMAN PATEL*'s hand.*

EESHWAR. How wonderful! It's good to see you both.

LAXMAN. I hope we haven't disturbed you?

EESHWAR. Not at all. I was just saying to Lopa, we don't see enough of people . . .

LOPA. Come, sit.

LATA. Thank you.

> LATA *sits down, and gives* LAXMAN *a look that says* 'Go on, tell them.'

> *Pause.*

LAXMAN. You're alone . . . ? I mean, nobody else in the house?

LOPA. Jai's taken Vina to the pictures and Atul's working.

LAXMAN. Good.

LATA. It's best that it's just us.

LOPA. Oh . . .

EESHWAR. Would you like some chai? How about a soft drink – orange, Coke, dandelion and burdock?

LATA. Not just now, thank you, Mr Dutt.

EESHWAR. Something stronger maybe?

LAXMAN. Nothing at all, thanks.

LOPA. They don't want anything.

EESHWAR. Nonsense! Lopa, put the kettle on. We'll have some tea.

LAXMAN. We just had some . . . before we came round to see you.

> *Silence.*

LATA. You must be wondering what it is we've come to see you about.

EESHWAR. You don't need an excuse to come and visit. We're practically family now.

LAXMAN. The thing is –

EESHWAR. Visiting is part of our culture. Every weekend I see cars filled with Asian families visiting!

Silence.

We're the visiting type – Indians.

Beat.

LATA. Should I tell them or do you want to do it?

LAXMAN. Well . . . you spoke to her first . . .

LOPA. Is something wrong?

LATA. We thought it right that you should both be informed . . . as Atul's parents . . .

LAXMAN. And I thought it best we all sit and discuss what to do about it.

LOPA. About what?

LATA. You know I called round this morning?

LOPA. Yes.

EESHWAR. Did she?

LOPA. Yes.

EESHWAR. You didn't tell me.

LOPA. Shh . . .

EESHWAR. Visitors, twice in one day.

LATA. Well . . . I had an intimate chat with Vina. And certain things came out of it.

EESHWAR. Came out of what?

LOPA *looks at him*.

LOPA. The chat . . .

She turns back to the PATELS.

What things exactly?

LAXMAN. When I got here, my Vina cried in my arms.

EESHWAR. You were visiting as well?

LAXMAN. She was so upset, she wanted to come back home.

LATA. She changed her mind in the end. She decided to stick it out, for Atul's sake.

LOPA. Stick what out?

LOPA *and* EESHWAR *exchange a look*.

LATA. It's about their marriage.

She turns to LAXMAN.

This would be better coming from you.

LAXMAN. No, no . . . you carry on. Woman to woman. This bit's best this way.

Pause.

LATA. It hasn't happened yet . . . You know what I'm saying?

LOPA. You don't mean? . . . That can't be true.

LATA. Just what I said.

LAXMAN. But it is.

LOPA *is not fazed by this news*. *It just confirms her suspicions that something was wrong*.

LOPA. Well . . . that explains a lot. No wonder they haven't been sleeping.

EESHWAR (*bewildered*). What's not happened yet? And who's not sleeping?

LOPA. Atul and Vina.

EESHWAR. I wish someone would tell me what the hell you're all talking about!

LATA. My daughter's not a woman yet, Mr Dutt.

EESHWAR *still looks quizzical*.

LOPA. He still doesn't get it.

LAXMAN. She's like she was, when she was a girl. She's still intact.

EESHWAR *looks to* LOPA *for an answer.*

LOPA. There's been no new planting in the Shalimar gardens since Vina came to live with us! She's still a virgin. Now do you understand?

EESHWAR *is gobsmacked*.

EESHWAR. Do you mean to say . . .

LAXMAN. Exactly.

EESHWAR. He hasn't . . .

LAXMAN. No.

EESHWAR. After six weeks!

LOPA. Is she sure?

LATA. They've done other things . . . but not the rest.

LOPA. And she'd know if he'd done the rest.

EESHWAR. Well, I don't know what to say.

LOPA. In that case, don't say anything.

EESHWAR. How can I stay quiet about something like this?

LATA. I understand how you must feel, Mr Dutt. You are his father, after all.

EESHWAR. It's the disgrace.

LOPA. What disgrace?

EESHWAR. Suppose it leaked out in the factory.

LOPA. It's got nothing to do with anyone else. This is about
    Atul and Vina.

EESHWAR. I've worked in that factory for twenty-nine years.
    I've a reputation to keep. If this got out, I'd be a laughing
    stock. *Hai Ram!* To think a son of mine couldn't prove his
    manhood!

LOPA. Oh, so that's how you prove it, is it?

EESHWAR. How else is there?

LAXMAN. What are we going to do? That's the question.

LOPA. Well, you can't stand over him and force the boy to
    do it.

EESHWAR. Lopa!

LOPA. They'll get to it eventually . . .

EESHWAR. If it hasn't happened in six weeks – and we've
    had no telly for three, so there's nothing been stopping
    them – then I don't think it's going to happen at all!

LATA. It's true. The longer a man goes without working up to
    it, the less likely he is to start.

LAXMAN. Lata!

LATA. It's an instinct . . . and an instinct is nothing if it isn't
    working.

    She glances at LAXMAN.

    You don't get husbands doing that kind of thing out of pity.

LOPA. True. Pleasure or nothing for a man.

LATA. They hate facing up to things, in case they discover
    their own weaknesses.

LAXMAN. What weaknesses would they be, Lata?

EESHWAR *notices the tension building between the*
PATELS.

EESHWAR. No use blaming each other for this. It's nobody's
fault . . .

LAXMAN. We have to find some sort of solution.

LOPA. What do you have in mind, Mr Patel?

LATA. I need to have another good talk to Vina. Find out more
details.

LAXMAN. I think she'd rather have a talk with me . . .

LATA. I'll deal with it. She won't be honest with you. Maybe
you should speak to Atul, Mr Dutt?

EESHWAR. Me? I've never had a proper talk to him in his
life. He won't listen to me.

LOPA. A nice thing for a father to say!

EESHWAR. You talk to him.

LOPA. It's not a mother's duty.

EESHWAR. He always turns to you . . . He's never bothered
with me.

LOPA. That's because he thinks you've never understood him.
Or want to.

EESHWAR. It's not that . . . We've just always . . .

LAXMAN. It's only natural that a son should turn to his
mother. Just as a daughter will turn to her father.

LATA *looks at him, but he avoids her glance.*

EESHWAR. Achaa . . . but on the other hand, you get the sort
of man that's spent too much time with their mothers.

LOPA. What's that supposed to mean?

EESHWAR *and* LAXMAN *exchange looks.*

LAXMAN. Has . . . Atul knocked about with girls much?

LOPA. Good girls don't knock about with boys, Mr Patel. And good boys don't knock about with girls that do.

LAXMAN. I mean . . . did he have much of a social life before he met Vina?

EESHWAR (*accusingly*). He's a member of the Classic Indian Film Club.

LATA. Achaa!

LAXMAN. And does he like to keep fit?

LOPA. No. He'd come home from work, eat, then go upstairs and listen to his music.

EESHWAR. Chamber music and that bloody film *Pakeeza* lies at the bottom of all this.

LATA. *Pakeeza*?

EESHWAR. Yes. I knew something was wrong when he stopped doing the bhangra!

LOPA. What's that got to do with it?

EESHWAR. What hot-blooded Indian male doesn't do the bloody bhangra? It's a manly dance!

LOPA. Oh, shut up! If you can't say anything sensible don't say anything at all. No one's marriage starts off perfectly.

She gives EESHWAR *a look*.

But some people don't like to admit these things. And I'm talking from experience.

EESHWAR. I beg your pardon?

LOPA. I said, I was talking from experience.

EESHWAR. I might not be Shashi Kapoor in the Romeo stakes, but there's nothing odd or queer about me!

Silence.

LOPA. What do you mean by that?

EESHWAR. What I said. That son of yours has brought shame on this family! All his fancy music and reading and fancy bloody talk and when it comes to it, he can't fulfil his married duties. There's something very odd, very queer about that.

EESHWAR goes over to the fireplace and starts to fill his pipe. LOPA is very angry, but contains it.

Pause.

LOPA. Tell me, Mr and Mrs Patel . . . Would you say there was anything odd or queer about a man who goes on his honeymoon and takes his best friend with him?

The PATELS smile. EESHWAR turns to face LOPA.

LATA. A friend . . . you mean another man?

LAXMAN. What would you want your friend on your honeymoon for?

EESHWAR. But I didn't take him on the honeymoon, Lopa.

LOPA. We all travelled on the same train to Blackpool, didn't we? Same compartment. You two sat next to each other laughing all the way.

EESHWAR. It was the first holiday we'd taken in six years of being over here.

LOPA. Then in Blackpool we all got in a cab together and went to the same hotel. 'Honeymoon Villas'.

EESHWAR. I couldn't ask Brijesh to find another place by himself.

LOPA. Then, that first night, we all went to the Pleasure Beach together.

EESHWAR. How could we leave him alone in the hotel? Didn't we all have a good time walking along the front?

LOPA. Then I stood and watched them on the bumper cars, the Big Dipper, the ghost train, the waltzers . . . the tunnel of love.

LATA. The what?

EESHWAR. We thought they were speedboats.

LOPA. You should have seen the pair of them, sat there with all those other couples. Having their photos taken of the happy event.

EESHWAR. You said you didn't like the rides . . . that they made you feel sick.

LOPA. Then back at the hotel we had a romantic candlelit meal for three.

EESHWAR. I couldn't let him sit at a table on his own. People would have thought he was odd.

LOPA. How odd do you think the three of us looked, sat together at the honeymoon table by the window?

EESHWAR. He had his own bedroom and we had ours. What more do you want?

LAXMAN. It looks a bit odd if you look at it as an outsider, Mr Dutt. I know he was your best friend . . .

EESHWAR. He was more than that . . . he meant the world to me, that lad. We'd worked solidly, never spending a penny on ourselves. It all went back to our families. I'd only just married, before I came over. But me and Brijesh pooled what was left of our savings and I brought Lopa here to join me. It was Brijesh's idea that I took Lopa on a honeymoon. I couldn't leave him behind on his own . . .

LATA. But all the same . . .

Pause.

EESHWAR. No. He had to come . . . after all the work . . . He deserved it too. Ahh, but we looked slick that week, yaar! We went to Burtons and bought safari suits. Lightweight, non-crease, built-in belt, lovely they were.

LOPA. Very smart.

EESHWAR. I wore misty blue and Brijesh wore purple. I'll never forget it.

LOPA. They liked to go off for a walk along the front before dinner.

LATA. Without you?

LOPA. I used to watch them from the window.

EESHWAR. We always went for walks. We used to go on the moors here. I saw no reason to stop because we were in Blackpool.

LATA. You left your wife, who you hadn't seen for two years, alone in the hotel?

LOPA. It was all new to me . . . we'd hardly spent any time together before Eeshwar went off to England.

EESHWAR. I tell you, we looked like a couple of bloody film stars! You should have seen the way people parted as we walked along. Just moved to either side . . . They'd never seen Indians dressed like us before. Some of them didn't like it either, but we didn't care. Not any more.

He takes out an imaginary comb and runs it through his hair.

We just walked along that front, through those crowds, looking like a million dollars! Amitabh Bachchan and Rajesh Khanna do Blackpool! I was Amitabh, of course.

Beat.

I'll never forget that moment for as long as I live . . . It was the highlight of my week.

LATA. Walking along the front in Blackpool with your friend on your honeymoon?

She looks to LOPA, *who shrugs resignedly.*

EESHWAR. You have to remember the moments when life hands them to you, Mrs Patel. No matter how inappropriate they may be. You have to grab them and cherish them. Isn't that right, Mr Patel?

LAXMAN (*sadly*). I've forgotten any I ever had.

LOPA. Then they'd come back and we'd all sit and have dinner.

EESHWAR. What was wrong with that?

LOPA. I don't know. But however you look at a honeymoon for three – and there's more than one way you can look at it – it must have seemed a bit queer to people watching.

EESHWAR. I never once, in all the years I knew Brijesh . . . ever saw him in that way!

LOPA. I never said you did.

EESHWAR. It's been twenty-eight years since all that happened, Lopa. Why are you suggesting that now?

LOPA. I'm not suggesting anything. I'm just telling you how things looked.

Pause.

You're a good man, Eeshwar . . . a kind man in your own way. But sometimes you can be such a bloody fool . . . Atul is no more odd or queer than you and Brijesh were.

LATA. No one thought . . .

LOPA. And even if he was gay, which is what you're all suggesting, then it still wouldn't matter. Nature would have done it. And nature knows what she's doing. And it's a father's duty to protect a boy like that, since it must have come through the father or mother. Not be shamed by it and turn on him like the rest of the mob.

Pause.

LATA. What happened to him?

EESHWAR. Who?

LATA. Brijesh?

EESHWAR. Brijesh? . . . Oh . . . people . . . you know . . .

He looks unsure.

I'm going to pop to the off-licence. Will you have a drink, Mr Patel?

LAXMAN *looks at* LATA.

LAXMAN. Yes. I will, thank you, Mr Dutt.

EESHWAR *puts on his jacket and heads for the door. He stops and turns to* LOPA.

EESHWAR. Having you in England, after all the waiting . . . I'd never been so happy in my life. It felt only natural that I share that with my best friend.

He exits, watched by LOPA. *She walks over and gets a couple of glasses from a cabinet. She takes a cloth from a drawer and starts to polish them.*

LOPA. He used to come round here all the time when I first came over.

She turns and looks at the PATELS.

Brijesh . . . he and Eeshwar would play cards or maybe sing together. They were like two schoolboys the way they joked with each other. He was very good with his hands, always making things for us. Shelves and cupboards, he made the shelving for that shrine . . .

LATA. Very nice finish.

LOPA. One evening he came over as usual. It was May . . . Such a beautiful warm evening. I was trying to paint the ceiling upstairs and making a mess of it, but I was enjoying myself. Eeshwar was working late. So I asked Brijesh to help me, while he waited. He was holding the ladder. I kept splashing him. It was an accident at first . . . but then I started to do it on purpose . . . I was a silly girl, only just turned eighteen, and it was fun. And he was acting so stern and serious. It made me laugh to watch him. He got so worked up, but he didn't say a word . . . He was very shy. This made me laugh even more. I remember it like it was yesterday.

Pause.

LAXMAN. What happened then?

LOPA. Then?

LATA. You were painting upstairs.

LOPA. Oh, he didn't wait for Eeshwar, he went home before he got back. He didn't come round the following night, or the night after that . . . Do you know, I've not seen him from that day to this.

LAXMAN. Didn't Eeshwar go and ask why?

LOPA. He wanted to, but I wouldn't let him. I don't know if that was the right decision now, but I thought it was at the time.

LAXMAN. But they were best friends . . .

LOPA. And I was a young wife. With a woman the home comes first . . . not friendship. Besides, I was here now.

LAXMAN. How sad.

LOPA. I can't tell you how empty this little house felt on those evenings, without him . . . He moved south, to work in a motor-car factory. Eeshwar was broken-hearted. He tried not to show it, but I could see. He never wrote much . . . and eventually, not at all. Then Atul came along and Eeshwar had something to come home and play with again. And Brijesh . . . he became one of Eeshwar's moments . . .

EESHWAR *comes back, carrying a bottle of whisky.*

LOPA. You were quick.

EESHWAR. He always serves me first. Not a bad lad, for a Nazi.

EESHWAR *opens the bottle and pours a drink for* LAXMAN.

EESHWAR. Mrs Patel?

LATA. Oh, good heavens no, not for me.

EESHWAR. You sure . . . ?

He looks to LOPA.

Lopa?

LOPA. Yes, why not? It's been one of those nights.

LAXMAN *gives his glass a squirt from a soda syphon.*

LATA. I was just thinking, perhaps Vina could go and see my brother-in-law about this.

LOPA. The nurse?

LATA. He's practically a doctor.

LAXMAN. He's got a white coat and a tongue-scraper. He's hardly Professor Lord Winston.

LATA. Maybe he could advise her on things we can't.

LAXMAN. He can't give her any more advice than I could, and I'm her father.

LATA. He's involved in medicine. Maybe there's something he could give her to help.

LAXMAN. She doesn't need to take anything like that.

LATA. There are oils and things he might be able to suggest.

LAXMAN (*dismissively*). Nonsense. If she needs to see a doctor, she can go to a proper one. My brother's all right for the odd ache or indigestion, but this is quite different . . .

He turns away from LATA *and addresses* EESHWAR *and* LOPA.

Maybe the first thing for both of them should be a thorough check-up from people who know about these things . . .

LATA (*angry*). You wouldn't care if Vina was a virgin at ninety!

The others are shocked at this outburst.

LAXMAN. What did you say?

LATA. You heard me. You've never wanted her to grow up.

LAXMAN. How can –

LATA. Don't interrupt me now.

> EESHWAR *and* LOPA *exchange a look.*

I'm saying what I want to say. What I should have said a long time ago and never could, because I was always shut out!

LAXMAN. If you were, it was all your own fault. You never had any time for her!

LATA. I was always there. You didn't give me a chance!

LAXMAN. You did nothing but criticise her.

LATA. I wanted what was best . . .

LAXMAN. For her or for you? What about her hair, eh? Was that what was best for her?

EESHWAR. Her hair?

> LOPA *gives* EESHWAR *a shove to shut him up.* LAXMAN *knocks back his drink and pours himself another, to* EESHWAR*'s surprise.* EESHWAR *is about to give him a squirt from the soda syphon, but* LAXMAN *just knocks it back, then pours himself another.* EESHWAR *raises his eyebrows to* LOPA.

LAXMAN. I'll tell you why you're so upset. It's because of guilt. You feel guilty! After all these years you're beginning to feel it!

LATA. Why should I feel guilty?

LAXMAN. Because it was you who convinced her to get married so quickly.

LATA. I wanted her to be happy.

LAXMAN. You wanted her out of the house! Away from her home – away from me.

LATA. That isn't true.

LAXMAN. You thought I'd be so lost without her around that I'd turn to you . . . Well, it hasn't worked out that way, has it?

LOPA. *Bas*, *bas*, *bas* . . . Let's not talk any more about it . . .

EESHWAR. What about her hair?

LAXMAN. When Vina was young, she used to have two lovely long plaits. People used to stop and look at her in the street. You'd hear them say how beautiful she looked.

LATA. She was bullied. The other children used to call her 'Paki' because of them . . .

LAXMAN. She used to like me to comb her hair and put in her plaits before she went to bed. Ever since she was tiny . . .

LATA. She was getting too close to you. It's not healthy for a girl of that age to get too close to her father.

LAXMAN. What has the world become when a girl can't show love to her father?

LOPA. *Haan!* All love's fallen under suspicion these days.

LAXMAN. How can you say that to me, Lata? How could you even suggest . . .

LATA (*distressed*). I . . . I just meant she needed to spend a bit more time with me . . . especially then. What did you know about being a young woman?

LAXMAN *pours himself another drink.*

Pause.

EESHWAR. And is that it? She had lovely plaits?

LAXMAN *looks over at* LATA.

LAXMAN. I came home from work one day. Sat down and ate. I could hear whispering from the kitchen. Then Vina came into the lounge. I almost didn't recognise her. Her hair was short and frizzy . . . she'd had it cut and permed or something. I was so shocked . . . I couldn't speak. I felt so angry. Vina just cried . . . She just fell into my arms and cried . . . 'I'm sorry, Daddy,' she kept saying. 'I'm so sorry.'

He turns to LATA.

And you – standing there . . . 'Don't blame her,' you said. 'It was me. I persuaded her.' There was such defiance in your voice, Lata. You'd gone out of your way just to spite me. To use our little girl like that . . . I admit, it worked . . . you hurt me – deeply. But I haven't bothered you much since, have I?

LATA (*very upset*). I'm sorry . . . I'm so sorry . . .

Scene Two

ATUL*'s bedroom. That night.*

ATUL *gets out of bed and wanders over to the window. He stands for a moment, looking out. He looks back at* VINA, *asleep in bed. He heads out of the door and downstairs.*

EESHWAR *and* LOPA*'s bedroom.*

LOPA *wakes. She hears* ATUL *going down the stairs. She gives* EESHWAR *a shove.*

LOPA. Eeshwar! Eeshwar! Wake up!

EESHWAR. What is it? What?

LOPA. It's Atul . . . He's gone downstairs . . .

   ATUL *goes through to the kitchen.*

EESHWAR. What?

LOPA. Atul's gone downstairs.

EESHWAR. You woke me to tell me that?

LOPA. Up! *Chelo!* . . . This is the perfect time for you to go and have a word with him.

EESHWAR glances over at the clock.

EESHWAR. Oh, *poggle*! It's the middle of the bloody night, woman!

LOPA jumps up and gets his dressing gown.

LOPA. Best to do it now, while no one's around.

EESHWAR is sitting on the side of the bed now, putting on his slippers.

EESHWAR. I'm around. What makes you think I want to talk about it?

LOPA helps him into his dressing gown.

I'm not so sure this is best coming from me.

LOPA. You're his father.

EESHWAR. Precisely . . . I'm his father and . . . and he is proof of my working mechanism. It'll be like rubbing his face in it.

LOPA. Rubbish!

She hurries him over to the door.

EESHWAR. But I've never spoken to anyone about these things before.

LOPA. He isn't anyone. He's your son and he needs your help.

EESHWAR. I've never seen another man naked.

LOPA. You're going to talk to him, not give him an examination!

She pushes EESHWAR through the door and closes it behind him. EESHWAR hovers about near the top of the stairs. Then decides to head down. He pretends to clear his throat.

Living room.

EESHWAR *pops his head into the room, looking for* ATUL.
*He goes over to the mantelpiece. He takes his pipe, which he
nervously starts to clean and fill with tobacco.* ATUL *comes in,
holding a cup of tea and the radio, which is playing. He stops
and looks at his father.*

EESHWAR. I . . . I . . . didn't hear you up, son.

ATUL. I couldn't sleep.

EESHWAR. No. Nor could I . . . Something on your mind?

ATUL. No . . . just woke and fancied a cup of tea. You?

EESHWAR. No . . . No, nothing. I put it down to your
mother's onion bhajis . . .

He taps his chest and screws up his face.

Bit repetitive.

Pause.

ATUL. Right then . . . Better try and get my head down.

Desperate to get away, ATUL *makes for the stairs.*

EESHWAR. Well, don't run off . . .

ATUL *stops.*

ATUL. No?

EESHWAR. We . . . we could have a chat . . .

ATUL. About what?

EESHWAR. Anything . . . It may help us feel sleepy.

ATUL *puts his tea and the radio down on the table and
looks up expectantly, waiting for* EESHWAR *to begin the
chat.*

Pause.

What?

ATUL. I'm waiting for the chat to start.

EESHWAR. Well, I don't mean anything in particular! Just . . . chit-chatting . . . about things –

ATUL. What things?

EESHWAR. I don't know, any bloody thing!

ATUL. I'll go to bed if you're going to start shouting.

EESHWAR. All I'm suggesting is, we pass a little time away in conversation, until one or either of us feels sleepy again. Is that too much to ask?

ATUL. All right . . . Erm . . . What do you think about India having the nuclear bomb?

EESHWAR. I don't care about India and its nuclear bloody bombs.

ATUL. You've got relatives there.

EESHWAR. None that I like.

Pause.

How's . . . the cinema?

ATUL. Good. The cinema's good. The kiosk's started selling Haribo sweets. My particular favourites are Tangfastics. I suggested a bit of new carpet for the projection room, but we just can't decide on whether it should be plain or patterned.

EESHWAR. Why's it so difficult for us to talk?

Pause.

ATUL. You've never wanted to before.

EESHWAR. That's not what I asked. Why do we always end up bickering . . . ?

ATUL. I'm going back to bed.

ATUL *gathers his things and heads for the stairs.*

EESHWAR. Don't go . . . stay . . .

ATUL *stops and turns back to* EESHWAR.

ATUL. We don't talk because I've never believed you were
ever interested in anything I had to say.

EESHWAR. No, son, that's not –

ATUL. Let me finish. You wanted to know why, and I'm going
to tell you. Why should I talk to you when all you've ever
done is sit there waiting to shoot me down, tell me how
wrong I am and go out of your way to make me look stupid
and ridiculous?

EESHWAR. That's not true.

ATUL. Yes, it is! And it's never bothered you who was there
to witness it. In fact, the bigger the audience, the more you
enjoy it. Talk to you! Talk to you! You've never stopped
telling me what a failure I am. How I'm never gonna
amount to anything. What a waste I'm making of the start
you gave me. How different you were at my age. How you
came here and made a success of it. Do you know something,
Dad? I don't care what you did! I don't care where you
came from! I don't care about the sacrifices you made
'cause it all amounts to nothing when you can't sit down
and talk without beating me over the head with it.

EESHWAR. I never meant to hurt you, son.

ATUL. I don't want to hear that now. It's not what I need . . .
It's too late for that . . .

EESHWAR. If there's anything I can do, son, to make –

ATUL. Nothing! You can't do anything for me now . . .
nothing!

ATUL *turns and goes up the stairs, slamming his bedroom
door shut.* LOPA *comes out of her room and heads down
the stairs to the living room.*

LOPA. Well, how did it go?

Beat.

EESHWAR. We chatted . . .

Scene Three

Living room. The next day.

ATUL *sits drinking tea at the table. Bollywood music plays from the radio.* ETASH *comes in, carrying two plates with kebab rolls on them.*

ETASH. *Aradhana*?

ATUL. Rajesh Khanna and Sharmila Tagore! *Dil se*!

ETASH. Hardly a classic!

ATUL. It's a modern classic.

ETASH. Doesn't count. *Mughal-e-Azam*?

ATUL. Dilip Kumar and Madhubala. *Junglee*?

ETASH. Shammi Kapoor and Saira Banu. *Kaagaz Ke Phool*?

ATUL. Sunnil Dutt and Waheeda Rehman! *Do Raaste*?

ETASH. Rajesh Khaana and Mumtaz. *Chaudhvin Ka Chand*?

ATUL *can't think.*

ATUL. Ahhhhhh! Erm . . . Nargis and Dev Anand?

ETASH. No!

ETASH *makes the clock sound from the TV show* Countdown.

I'm starting the clock . . . chink-ka-chack-ka-chick-ka-chink-ka-chink-ka-chack-chink-ka-chack-ka-chick-ka-chink-ka-chink-ka-chack . . .

ATUL. I'm not playing.

ETASH (*signalling that the time is up*). Do, do, do, do, diddle-le dum, booo!

ATUL. I said I wasn't playing. All right, who was it?

ETASH. Waheeda Rehman and Guru Dutt. You owe me twenty quid!

ATUL sits down, defeated. ETASH drops down to one knee and starts to sing and act out a love song from a Bollywood movie, using ATUL as his point of adoration.

ATUL. Oh, get lost!

JIVAJ BHATT appears from the kitchen, smoking a cigarette.

JIVAJ. Hello, ladies, not disturbing you, am I? The back door were open.

ATUL and ETASH stop messing around.

ATUL. I was just getting an abject lesson on classic Indian cinema.

JIVAJ. Is that what they call it these days . . . ?

ETASH. Calls himself a film buff, but he doesn't know his arse from his elbow.

ETASH ruffles ATUL's hair.

JIVAJ. Yeah, I heard he were fond of the classics. Shouldn't you be rewinding *Lakshya* for the seven-thirty . . .

ETASH. Yeah, all right, I'm on it. I've been doing the splicing all morning.

ATUL. We haven't finished our break yet.

JIVAJ. I don't pay you to sit about on your arse, singing to each other.

ATUL. Don't you?

JIVAJ. Not on my time.

ETASH grabs ATUL passionately.

ETASH. But how can I leave him! *Hai, bhagwaan!* Oh my love, come back to me. Oh, *mera mohabbat*! *Mein tum hai.*

Main tum hai, pyar kurta hai. Torn from my arms, by another woman!

JIVAJ (*muttered*). She'd probably hand him back, from what I've heard.

ATUL. What did you say?

JIVAJ. Nothing.

ATUL. If you've got something to say, say it to my face.

JIVAJ. Come on, get back to work. The pair of you.

JIVAJ *heads for the front door.* ATUL *jumps up and yanks him back by his shoulder.*

Hey, hey, hey, watch the hands . . .

ETASH *is shocked.*

ETASH. Atul!

ATUL. You just said something about my wife not bothering about me now . . .

JIVAJ. What's your problem?

ATUL. What you just said.

JIVAJ. What you getting so touchy about . . . ?

ATUL. You talkin' about my wife.

JIVAJ. It's not just me. Seems everyone's at it.

ETASH. Just leave him alone, Jivaj!

JIVAJ. I just heard a rumour, that's all.

ATUL. Heard what?

JIVAJ. That you're not getting on so well.

ATUL. Who told you that?

JIVAJ. Not true, is it? Is it?

Beat.

It is, isn't it?

He starts to laugh.

ETASH. What's not true?

JIVAJ. The bloody professor here –

ATUL. Shut your mouth, I said.

JIVAJ. Been married six weeks and he hasn't shagged his wife yet!

ATUL. Bastard!

ATUL *makes a grab for him and they start to wrestle.*
JIVAJ *manages to get behind* ATUL *and locks his arms so his face is right up against* ATUL's.

JIVAJ. Trying to be a man now, are you, Dutt? Bit too late for that now. I'll tell you what, though, you bring that little bit of *cheeni* up to my office and I'll do the job for you! I'll let you watch if you like . . . give you a few pointers.

ATUL *struggles to break free.*

ETASH. Get off him!

JIVAJ. I bet you'd like to see me on the job with her, wouldn't you? Yeah, you'd like that.

ATUL *throws his head back and butts* JIVAJ *in the face. He turns quickly and follows up with a kick to the groin.* JIVAJ *collapses to the floor.* ATUL *is on him in an instant. He straddles him, trying to strangle him.* ETASH *tries to stop him. There's knocking at the front door.*

ETASH. Atul, get off him!

ATUL. Do a job for me, would you? Let's see you do it now then! Come on, do it now!

ETASH. Atul, don't, you'll kill him!

ETASH *jumps up and opens the door.*

MOLLY. Is he still here?

ETASH. Molly, quick!

MOLLY BHATT *sees the fight and rushes in.*

MOLLY. What the frig d'you think you're doing? Get off him!

She gets to them and starts to pull ATUL *off* JIVAJ.

You're gonna choke him! Let go of him! Atul, let go, I said!

ETASH *and* MOLLY *manage to drag* ATUL *off* JIVAJ, *who staggers away coughing and spluttering.*

JIVAJ. He's gone mad! Call the police, he wants locking up! He nearly killed me!

ATUL. I'd have done it and all, if I'd wanted to. You're just not worth it.

MOLLY. Whatever's to do, Atul? What happened?

JIVAJ. He's sacked, that's what's happened! You get your stuff and get out of my cinema!

MOLLY. Is that what all this is about?

ETASH. He were saying dirty things about Vina, Molly . . .

JIVAJ. You shut it and get back to work, you!

ETASH. He said he'd do a job on her if Atul weren't man enough to do it!

MOLLY *realises what's happened.*

MOLLY. Ohhh, Atul love, I'm so sorry . . .

JIVAJ. You're finished, the pair of you . . . Should have seen what they were up to when I came in! Disgusting it were!

MOLLY *turns to* JIVAJ.

MOLLY. Haven't you done enough?

JIVAJ. He almost killed me . . .

MOLLY. You said you wouldn't breathe a word . . . I bet you couldn't wait to get back here and stick the boot in, could you?

JIVAJ. He were asking for it . . . You're finished, Dutt, do you hear me, finished!

ATUL. Stuff your job!

ATUL exits through the back. MOLLY *swings her bag at* JIVAJ, *hitting him across the head.*

JIVAJ. What was that for?

MOLLY. I should have let him choke the living daylights out of you, you weasly little bastard! You do a job for him? You couldn't do a job for our cat! You're all talk, you! I've a good mind to . . .

She starts to kick and whack him with her handbag. He backs out followed by MOLLY *and* ETASH.

You do a job! You wouldn't know where to start. You can't even do a job for me! Every waiter at the Gurkha Tandoori's been doing your job for years!

Scene Four

Kitchen. Later the same day.

EESHWAR i*s sitting at the table.* LOPA *puts some steaming curry on a dish and places it in front of him. He starts to help himself.*

EESHWAR. Lopa, chilli pickle is finished!

LOPA *passes him a jar and a chapatti basket. She pours him some water from a jug. She sits and watches as he spoons chilli pickle onto his food and mixes it in.*

LOPA. You look like you're mixing concrete.

EESHWAR. Do you mind minding your own business?

EESHWAR *puts a spoonful in his mouth and chews. He stops, and takes a glass of water.*

LOPA. I thought you'd put too much on.

EESHWAR. Not enough!

He adds more to the mix on his plate and breaks some roti to eat. ATUL *comes in. He looks very angry.* LOPA *is surprised to see him.*

LOPA. You're home early, *putter* . . . Are you feeling well?

ATUL *walks straight through and heads for the stairs.*

ATUL. Fine.

LOPA. Nothing wrong, is there?

EESHWAR (*without looking up from his food*). He's ill or he's got the sack.

ATUL *rushes up the stairs noisily. We hear the door to his bedroom slam.*

That'll be the sack.

LOPA. He looked upset.

EESHWAR. He should be, the way he spoke to me the other night.

LOPA. No, something's upset him.

EESHWAR. Why didn't you ask him?

LOPA. Why didn't you?

EESHWAR. I won't have him walking through my house like he was on his way to do *tutti* in a field!

LOPA. Don't be so vulgar! I'll take him some tea and ask him.

She starts to pour another cup.

EESHWAR. Don't mollycoddle him.

VINA *comes in.*

LOPA. Hello, *bete.*

VINA. Is Jai back yet?

EESHWAR. No, *bete*, why?

VINA. He's taking me out tonight.

LOPA. Atul's just come home.

VINA. Has he? Nothing's wrong, is there?

EESHWAR. He walked through here like he was going to do *tutti* in a field.

LOPA. Don't talk like that at the table.

VINA. Did he say anything?

LOPA. He seemed . . . a bit quiet.

She gives VINA *the tea.*

Why don't you take him this tea?

VINA*, looking worried, heads off up the stairs.*

ATUL*'s bedroom.*

ATUL *opens a suitcase on the bed. He starts to remove clothes from his drawer and wardrobe.* VINA *comes in.*

VINA. I've brought you a cup of tea, Atul. What are you doing?

He ignores her.

What's the matter? . . . Atul, I'm talking to you! What are you doing?

ATUL. I heard you the first time.

VINA. Then why don't you answer me?

ATUL. I've got nothing to say to you!

VINA. Atul, don't! Stop it! Stop it!

She tries to stop him packing. He pushes her away.

Why are you doing this?

ATUL. I'm getting away from you!

VINA. I don't understand . . .

ATUL. It's simple . . . I'm leaving you. Do you understand
    that?

VINA. Why? What have I done?

ATUL. You opened your big mouth!

VINA. I haven't!

ATUL. I asked you not to tell anybody. I begged you!

VINA. But I haven't . . .

ATUL. You're a liar!

VINA. I . . . I got upset – my mum was here. She . . .

ATUL. And your dad!

VINA. What was I supposed to do?

ATUL. That's what you were all yapping about the other day,
    wasn't it?

VINA. I needed to talk to someone!

ATUL. Why didn't you talk to me?

VINA. Because you've stopped listening to me! We can't talk
    about anything any more without you blowing your top.
    I just can't carry on like this . . . pretending everything's
    fine, when it isn't. Don't you think nobody can see
    something's wrong?

ATUL. You've changed your tune. I thought you said it didn't
    matter.

VINA. It didn't. It's you! . . . You're not the same any more,
    Atul . . . You look at me with such hatred sometimes. As if
    it was all my fault. I don't know what I've done . . .

ATUL. You've made me into a bloody laughing stock round
    here, that's what you've done! I might not have made a

good start to our marriage, but I didn't expect you to go round discussing our sex life with everyone!

VINA. I haven't!

ATUL. You haven't? Then how come Jivaj Bhatt said he'd do a job for me, with my wife, if I couldn't manage it?

VINA. Oh, Atul . . . I'm so sorry . . . I didn't tell anybody else, I swear!

ATUL. You didn't have to, you stupid cow, you told your mother! That was enough!

VINA is very upset.

VINA. I love you, I wouldn't do anything to hurt you . . .

ATUL. You're a liar! You're a bloody little liar!

He pushes his face right up against hers.

Did you tell 'em everything, did you? All the gory details! Tell 'em how you always put me off! How you laughed at me on our wedding night! Did you say that, did you! Did you? Well, did you?

VINA suddenly slaps him across the face. ATUL is shocked. He grabs hold of her roughly.

You bloody little bitch, I'll . . .

VINA (*defiantly*). You'll what?

They stand there looking at each other.

Living room.

EESHWAR *and* LOPA *are both sitting at the table.* EESHWAR *is still eating. They look up at the ceiling, then to each other.*

EESHWAR. Did you hear that?

LOPA. I heard nothing.

EESHWAR. I could have sworn I heard something.

LOPA. You're hearing things.

EESHWAR. It's funny Vina and Atul haven't come back down yet.

The door opens and JAI *comes in, taking off his helmet. He has a large parcel, wrapped loosely.*

JAI. Evening, parents! Vina home yet?

LOPA. She's upstairs.

JAI. Upstairs.

EESHWAR. Yes. Upstairs.

JAI *heads towards the stairs.*

LOPA. Where d'you think you are going?

JAI. Tell Vina I'm back. We're off out tonight. It's a Bombay Fever night at the Roxy.

LOPA. Don't.

JAI. Don't what?

LOPA. Don't disturb her.

JAI. I won't.

LOPA. Her husband's with her.

JAI. Her what's with her?

LOPA. Oh, *bevacoof*! I said 'her husband'. Atul!

JAI. Oh, him. What's he doing home so early?

LOPA. Minding his own business. Like you should be.

EESHWAR. He walked through here like he was going to do *tutti* in a field.

LOPA. I warned you about that . . .

EESHWAR. There's no other way of putting it. He looked neither left or right.

JAI. D'you think he's got the sack, Dad?

EESHWAR. Not my business. But he's got no right to walk through here like he was . . .

He looks at LOPA. *She looks daggers at him.*

Well, he did!

JAI. I think I'll . . .

He heads for the stairs again. This time, LOPA *shoves him back in his seat.*

LOPA. You stay where you are. Eat, it's your favourite.

She moves a plate in front of him and starts to dollop food onto it.

JAI. Just give her a shout . . . let her know I'm here.

LOPA. She doesn't need to know you're here.

JAI. How do you know? She's looking forward to tonight.

LOPA. I've got a feeling. Ever had one? Besides, as I said, she's with her husband.

EESHWAR. Eat up, *putter*. You can't get the better of your mother. What's in the parcel?

JAI. They're lovebirds. A bloke at college breeds them.

EESHWAR. Really? Birds?

JAI. Want a look?

EESHWAR. Yes, why not? Move the plates, Lopa . . .

JAI *gets the parcel and removes the paper carefully. The birds start to sing.*

Are they for the house?

JAI. I got 'em for Vina and Atul . . .

LOPA. Oh, how pretty they are! What beautiful colours . . .

EESHWAR. They're lovely, aren't they?

JAI. I'll take 'em up and show them.

LOPA. Sit. They'll be down in their own time.

EESHWAR. Will they breed, son? Maybe we could have one
of the chicks, eh, Lopa?

LOPA. No, no, they won't. Not in captivity.

The doorbell rings.

EESHWAR. Visitors? I've barely finished my dinner.

The doorbell rings again.

Doorbell, Lopa . . . Best cover them up, son.

LOPA *goes to the door and opens it. It's* LATA PATEL.

LOPA. Hello, Mrs Patel. Eeshwar, Mrs Patel is here!

EESHWAR. Come along in, Mrs Patel, I was just saying to
Lopa, we're open house on a weekend.

LATA. Don't let me disturb you. Hello, Mr Dutt, Jai. My
husband just called to tell me that he's bumped into a friend
of his who's going back to India and wants a quick sale on
his house. Three bedrooms, £150,000 . . . But he needs a
quick answer.

EESHWAR. They haven't got that kind of money.

LOPA. Don't be so quick.

EESHWAR. Well, they haven't, and Atul won't go into debt.

LOPA. Where is it, Mrs Patel?

LATA. Near Bellhill Reservoir.

JAI. I know it, up Bellhill Brew. Not many Asians living round
there.

LOPA. Perfect for Atul, then.

LATA. He said it needs some work doing on it. But it's
liveable.

LOPA *goes over to* EESHWAR.

LOPA. Would you take a look at it, Eeshwar? Tea, Mrs Patel?

LATA. Yes, please.

EESHWAR. What's the use? Atul never takes any notice of me.

LATA. Where's Vina?

JAI. She's upstairs. I'll give her a shout. Tell her you're here.

He heads for the stairs again.

LOPA. You leave them alone.

LATA. Is anything wrong?

LOPA. Atul's with her.

LATA. Why's he home so early?

EESHWAR. He never said. He walked through here like he was going to do *tut* –

LOPA *picks up the teapot and shows it to* EESHWAR.

JAI. Give her a shout, Mrs Patel. I'm supposed to be taking her out tonight.

LATA. Well, it'll be a pity to miss that and the house. Don't you think, Mrs Dutt?

LOPA *turns to* JAI.

LOPA. You're like all single people. No respect for married couples.

LOPA *turns and gives* LATA *a very significant look to the ceiling.*

Once you get married you don't want anyone to come barging into your room any hour of the day.

LATA *looks puzzled for a moment. Then slowly the significance starts to sink in. She looks back at* LOPA, *who gives her another nod.*

LATA. It's practically monsoon weather out there.

It's now JAI*'s turn to look puzzled.*

EESHWAR. Did you get caught in it? I thought it was going to come down.

LATA. Yes. I said to Laxman earlier. Take your umbrella, it's going to rain.

EESHWAR. It got very dark, didn't it? I felt a few spots before I got in.

LATA. You can never tell with just a few spots of wet, what they are or where they've come from. Sometimes I've felt them when nobody else has.

EESHWAR. True. The odd spots can be anything. More than a few and you can bet it's rain. And if it has that telltale heaviness . . . you've got a monsoon.

JAI. Well . . . if it's following you about.

EESHWAR. Pardon?

JAI. If the wet follows you about, it's bound to be rain.

EESHWAR. You're too late, *putter*. That's the conclusion I've just reached with Mrs Patel.

The doorbell rings. EESHWAR *is about to tell* LOPA.

LOPA. I heard.

She opens the door. LAXMAN *comes in. He's folding up his umbrella.*

Oh, come in out of the rain, Mr Patel.

LAXMAN. Hello, Mrs Dutt, Mr Dutt, Jai . . .

LATA *gets up and helps her husband off with his coat as* LOPA *takes his umbrella into the kitchen and returns.*

Did you tell her about the house?

LATA. Who?

LAXMAN. Vina. We need an answer quickly.

LATA. She's upstairs.

LAXMAN. What's she doing there? Call her down quick!

JAI. I will, Mr Patel.

LOPA. You sit.

JAI. Mum, Mr Patel wants to tell her about the house!

LOPA. Well, I don't think Vina wants to see Mr Patel either.

LAXMAN. Well, it'll be the first time in her life that she doesn't.

LOPA. There has to be a first time for everything.

LATA. Just what I was thinking.

EESHWAR. Has it blown over?

LAXMAN. Has what blown over?

JAI. Oh, man, not this again!

LAXMAN. Why don't I go round to the cinema and tell Atul.

LATA. He isn't there.

LAXMAN. Where is he?

EESHWAR. He's upstairs with Vina.

LAXMAN. What's he doing home from work?

EESHWAR. He didn't say. He just walked through here like he was going to do –

JAI. They're coming down.

> ATUL *and* VINA *come down the stairs.* ATUL *is carrying a couple of cases.* VINA *is dressed up and carries her coat over her arm.*

I thought you were never coming down.

VINA. Hello, Mum – hello, Dad!

ATUL. All right, Mr and Mrs Patel . . .

LOPA. Did you get your cup of tea, son?

ATUL. Erm . . . yes, I did, thanks.

JAI. What's with the suitcases?

VINA. We're going on our honeymoon.

JAI. Where?

ATUL. Blackpool – eh, Vina?

VINA. Yes.

LATA. That's where your mummy and daddy went.

EESHWAR. Just the two of you?

VINA. I hope so.

LOPA. Has Jivaj given you the time off?

ATUL. He sacked me.

LOPA. What for?

ATUL. I tried to strangle him for not minding his own business.

LOPA. Maybe we should have some whisky after all. Eeshwar?

EESHWAR. I don't see why not. If they're off on their honeymoon . . . Will you have a drink before you go, son?

LOPA *looks at* ATUL. ATUL *smiles and looks back to his father.*

ATUL. I think I will, Dad. A bloke needs a drink when he's off on his honeymoon.

LOPA *takes the whisky and pours some glasses out.*

LATA. We've got some news for you both.

LAXMAN. There's a house going. Near Bellhill Reservoir.

ATUL. How much a month is it?

LAXMAN. It's for sale. It's £150,000.

VINA. That's a lot of money.

LATA. It's a bargain.

> LOPA *mumbles something to* ATUL.

ATUL. What do you think, Dad?

> EESHWAR *stands with his back to the room, as he fills his pipe by the fire. He turns.*

EESHWAR. Eh . . . ? Were you speaking to me, son?

ATUL. About this house. I'd like your advice before I did anything. I mean, you'd know better than anyone else. I've not had your experience . . .

> *They all look at* EESHWAR.

EESHWAR. My advice . . . What I say is, buy the bloody thing.

LOPA. That's right.

EESHWAR. You can't go wrong with bricks and mortar. Every young couple should have their own home, where they can feel at ease and happy.

JAI. Here, Vina, I got you these . . .

> JAI *puts the birdcage on the table.* VINA, *the* PATELS *and* LOPA *start cooing round the cage.* EESHWAR *walks over to* ATUL.

EESHWAR. What's your concern with the house?

ATUL. It's just the money that's the problem.

EESHWAR. Don't let money stand in the way. I've got a bit put aside . . . You just let me deal with the money side.

ATUL. Thanks very much, Dad, but I couldn't ask you . . .

EESHWAR (*gruffly, almost aggressively*). You're my son, aren't you? I'd be a damn poor father who couldn't help his own boy out.

ATUL. Ta, Dad . . . It's good to know I've got you behind me.

EESHWAR. Well . . . we all need someone . . .

VINA. Atul, have you seen these?

ATUL. They're lovely, Jai.

JAI. Pity you can't go on your honeymoon now.

LATA. Don't put it off now.

LOPA. No, you must go.

EESHWAR. Don't worry about the house. I'll look at it for you.

ATUL. If you would, Dad. I'll rely on your judgement.

EESHWAR. And if there's any plastering or painting to be done, then Jai will help out, won't you?

JAI. Oh, aye . . . and I'll look after these for you.

EESHWAR. Have you got a bit of cash?

ATUL. I'm all right, I've got me card.

EESHWAR *takes out his wallet and shoves a load of notes into* ATUL's *hand.*

EESHWAR. Here – it's the only way. Always have cash in your pocket.

ATUL. Thanks, Dad, I'll pay you back.

EESHWAR. Go on, off you go.

ATUL. Well, goodbye.

ATUL *holds out his hand.* EESHWAR *looks at it and takes it.*

EESHWAR. Goodbye son, and God bless . . .

ATUL *goes over and kisses* LOPA.

VINA. Goodbye, Mr Dutt, and thanks . . .

She gives him a hug and kiss. The PATELS *make to leave and join in with the goodbyes, as* ATUL *and* VINA *head out of the front door. Just before* ATUL *leaves, he turns and looks back at* EESHWAR. *He smiles at him, gives him a little wave and goes out to join the others.* EESHWAR, LOPA *and* JAI *are left in the room alone.*

JAI. I thought Atul looked different.

LOPA. He's a good boy.

EESHWAR *sits, almost dropping into a chair by the table.*

EESHWAR. You know who he reminded me of, Lopa? The way he turned and smiled as he went . . .

He can't bring himself to say his friend's name. He slowly drops his head. LOPA *puts a hand on his shoulder.*

JAI. Mum, what's up with Dad? He's crying!

EESHWAR. I can cry if I want, can't I?

He wipes the tears from his eyes.

It's life, son. It might make you laugh at your age, but one day it'll make you bloody cry.

The lights slowly fade, leaving only the glow from the shine until that too is swallowed up by the darkness, leaving the stage black.

The End.

Helen Edmundson
ANNA KARENINA *after* Tolstoy
THE CLEARING
CORAM BOY *after* Jamila Gavin
GONE TO EARTH *after* Mary Webb
THE MILL ON THE FLOSS *after* Eliot
MOTHER TERESA IS DEAD
WAR AND PEACE *after* Tolstoy

Stella Feehily
DUCK
O GO MY MAN

Debbie Tucker Green
BORN BAD
DIRTY BUTTERFLY
STONING MARY
TRADE & GENERATIONS

Ayub Khan-Din
EAST IS EAST
LAST DANCE AT DUM DUM
NOTES ON FALLING LEAVES

Tony Kushner
ANGELS IN AMERICA – PARTS ONE & TWO
CAROLINE, OR CHANGE
HOMEBODY/KABUL

Liz Lochhead
GOOD THINGS
MEDEA *after* Euripides
MISERYGUTS & TARTUFFE *after* Molière
PERFECT DAYS
THEBANS

Owen McCafferty
CLOSING TIME
DAYS OF WINE AND ROSES *after* JP Miller
MOJO MICKYBO
SCENES FROM THE BIG PICTURE
SHOOT THE CROW